NEW ENGLAND INSTITUTE
OF TECHNOLOGY
LIBRARY

A Skills and Strategies Handbook for Working with People

Robert J. Martin

Prentice-Hall, Inc., Englewood Cliffs, New Jersey 07632

Library of Congress Cataloging in Publication Data

Martin, Robert J. (date).
  A skills and strategies handbook for working with people.

  "A Spectrum Book."
  Bibliography: p.
  Includes index.
  1. Interpersonal relations. 2. Interpersonal communication. 3. Communication in personnel management. 4. Social skills. I. Title.
  HM132.M345 1983   302.3′4   83-4562
  ISBN 0-13-812370-5
  ISBN 0-13-812362-4 (pbk.)

Epigram from Von Foerster, Heinz, "On Constructing a Reality,"
in *Environmental Design Research,* Vol. 2, F. E. Preiser (ed.).
Copyright © 1973 by Dowden, Hutchinson & Ross, Inc.,
Stroudsburg, Pa. Reprinted by permission of the publisher and the author.

© 1983 by Prentice-Hall, Inc., Englewood Cliffs, New Jersey 07632.
All rights reserved. No part of this book may be reproduced in any form
or by any means without permission in writing from the publisher.
A Spectrum Book. Printed in the United States of America.

1 2 3 4 5 6 7 8 9 10

ISBN 0-13-812370-5
ISBN 0-13-812362-4 {PBK.}

Editorial/production supervision: Marlys Lehmann
Cover design © 1983 by Jeannette Jacobs
Manufacturing buyer: Edward J. Ellis

This book is available at a special discount when ordered in
bulk quantities. Contact Prentice-Hall, Inc., General
Publishing Division, Special Sales, Englewood Cliffs, N.J. 07632.

Prentice-Hall International, Inc., *London*
Prentice-Hall of Australia Pty. Limited, *Sydney*
Prentice-Hall Canada Inc., *Toronto*
Prentice-Hall of India Private Limited, *New Delhi*
Prentice-Hall of Japan, Inc., *Tokyo*
Prentice-Hall of Southeast Asia Pte. Ltd., *Singapore*
Whitehall Books Limited, *Wellington, New Zealand*
Editora Prentice-Hall do Brasil Ltda., *Rio de Janeiro*

Contents

Foreword by Don Dinkmeyer   *vii*

Preface   *ix*

Introduction:
Working effectively with people   *1*

part one
CHANGING "HELPFUL" RESPONSES TO EFFECTIVE RESPONSES   *7*

chapter one
Focusing on the problem
(instead of the person)   *11*

chapter two
Changing seven "helpful" responses
that don't work   *23*

part two
THE FIVE SKILLS   *33*

chapter three
Skill one: Giving feedback
by reflecting   *37*

chapter four
Skill two: Responding nonverbally
with attentive silence
and listening cues   *49*

chapter five
Skill three:
Asking for specifics   *58*

chapter six
Skill four: Making I-statements:
Getting across your own concerns,
needs, limits, and feelings   *73*

chapter seven
Skill five: Focusing on
an area of agreement   *86*

part three
**STRATEGIES FOR USING
THE SKILLS IN COMBINATION**   *93*

chapter eight
The five strategies   *95*

chapter nine
Strategy 1: Listening   *102*

chapter ten
Strategy 2: Helping others
think through problems by reflecting:
Non-directive problem solving   *108*

chapter eleven
Strategy 3: Getting others
to accept responsibility and make decisions:
Directive problem solving   *120*

chapter twelve
Strategy 4: Negotiating *137*

chapter thirteen
Strategy 5: Staying problem centered when attacked *150*

part four
AVOIDING TRAPS *163*

chapter fourteen
The trap of false responsibility *165*

chapter fifteen
Sorting out responsibility *175*

chapter sixteen
The pattern of powerlessness and how to avoid it *182*

chapter seventeen
Guidelines for using what you've learned *194*

References *202*

Appendix: Synopsis of the skills and strategies *205*

Index *215*

Foreword

A Skills and Strategies Handbook for Working with People focuses on a universal need—communication.

Ineffective communication reduces effectiveness in management, in the helping professions, in marriage, in parenting, and in all human relationships. Criticism, praise, guilt induction, reassurance, advice, positive thinking, sympathizing, logical arguments, and questioning are patterns used regularly in attempts to win the other person over to our way of thinking. Unfortunately these methods often leave others feeling inferior and inadequate. Robert Martin makes us aware of why these methods don't work and of what we can do about them. He shows us how to talk with people about what they do and how they can change.

Many books on communication end up giving the reader a potpourri of techniques without any direction. Robert Martin, in detail, helps us to see how to combine techniques into strategies for listening, helping others think through problems, getting others to take responsibility, negotiating, and resolving conflicts. The strength of this book lies in its variety of clearly illustrated skills and strategies. The examples help in the process of understanding, and the result is a practical methodology of human relations.

DR. DON DINKMEYER is the president
of the Communication and Motivation Training Institute,
Coral Springs, Florida.
He has a national and international reputation
as a consultant, psychologist, educator,
and author of twelve books.

The Ethical Imperative: Act always so as to increase the number of choices.

The Aesthetical Imperative: If you desire to see, learn how to act.

Heinz Von Foerster, 1973

Preface

"I knew about these skills before, but now I can use them." Knowing about the skills involved in working with people and using the skills effectively in everyday situations are very different things. This book teaches human relations skills in a way that bridges the gap between knowing about the skills and using them effectively.

Beginners will find a clear presentation of basic skills and dialogue examples that demonstrate their application to business, the helping professions, education, and interpersonal relationships. Readers familiar with the skills will find guidelines and strategies for organizing their skills into a systematic, powerful framework. Trainers and teachers of human relations skills, inevitably faced with people with a range of experience and sophistication, will find the content they expect of a book in this area presented in a way that stimulates all their students. The emphasis on demonstrating the techniques in combination and on showing how to choose the appropriate strategy for a particular situation is of particular interest because no other book does this.

The concepts and skills in this book derive from a variety of sources in the fields of communication, psychology, and human relations skills. Many of the ideas and techniques on which the skills and strategies are based have become so common that it is impossible to credit their origins. Wherever possible, pertinent sources are cited. The influence of the writings of the following people extends to the book as a whole: Rudolf Dreikurs, especially for his work on responsibility and equality in relationships; Carl Rogers and Thomas Gordon, for their writings on barriers to communication and listening techniques; William Glasser, for his approach to responsibility; and Albert Ellis, for his work on recognizing and changing irrational and self-defeating language.

ACKNOWLEDGMENTS

Thank you to all those in classes and workshops who used, discussed, and commented on the material in this book. Thanks especially to those who supplied examples; though to preserve their privacy their names are not given, their work is acknowledged in the text. My thanks also to the friends and colleagues who made suggestions and provided encouragement, especially Al Dye, Noah Hamilton, Dick Heun, Nancy Kiger, Paul Martin, Norm Wagner, and Art Wildhagen. John F. Feldhusen and Ernie McDaniels deserve special mention for their support while at Purdue University. Finally, for taking time out from working on a doctorate to read, comment, and edit, my thanks to Suzanne Martin.

**To my students: This book is the result
of working together and learning from one another**

Introduction: Working effectively with people

This is a book about interpersonal effectiveness. The essence of effectiveness is the ability to communicate and get a desired response from other people. Experiences of being effective with people include a wide variety of situations: confronting a certain person with a problem being caused by his or her behavior and working out a solution; being caught by surprise by an unexpected confrontation and feeling scared but reacting rationally; approaching another person and getting him or her to make a decision; expressing affection and having it returned. Such memories are usually of spontaneous, unplanned events. The challenge is to learn how to be effective when you want to be, as well as when you are spontaneously effective, and to be effective particularly in those situations in which you want change. Although it is hard work, the skills that result in being effective can be learned.

In working with other people—whether as a professional, business person, marriage partner, parent, or friend—there are situations in which we would like to be more effective—situations in which we talk when we should be listening, get stuck trying to solve someone else's problem, try to help someone think through a problem and end by feeling frustrated, want to ask for something and don't know how, or act defensive and say the wrong thing when criticized. Learning to be more effective in such situations requires four steps:

- Recognizing ineffective communication patterns
- Learning skills for effective communication
- Combining the skills effectively
- Recognizing and avoiding traps in using the skills

The book follows these four steps in its organization.

Part I shows how to recognize communications patterns that don't work. By identifying what doesn't work, you will be in a position to replace ineffective language with the skills presented in Part II.

Part II, the heart of the book, teaches five skills:

- *Reflecting*, that is, giving feedback by serving as a sounding board
- *Responding nonverbally* with attentive silence and listening cues
- *Asking for specifics* that clarify problems and what can be done about them
- Using *I-statements* to state your own wants, limits, needs, and feelings
- *Focusing on areas of agreement* when others attempt to engage you in a power struggle

You already use, in some form, the five skills—so much of the task of learning is becoming aware of, organizing, and then using what you already know.

Once you learn the skills, how do you use them effectively? Part III shows how to combine the skills into five strategies:

- Listening
- Helping others to think through problems
- Getting others to take responsibility and make decisions
- Negotiating when you have a problem
- Staying problem—centered when you are attacked or put on the defensive

The skills and strategies are necessary for being effective, but they are not always sufficient to avoid the pitfalls of working with other people. You need to know who is responsible for what, especially in problem-solving situations. No matter how skillful you are, if you take on responsibility for things over which you have no control, you won't be effective. The final section, Part IV shows how to avoid these traps.

Two Examples

The following examples will serve as snapshots of some of the territory we will cover. Many of the concepts and techniques covered in detail in later chapters are presented here by way of introduction. The first example is a dialogue based on a conversation that took place between myself and a building and equipment supervisor.

While attending a conference in Memphis, I needed a movable spotlight and a person to run it. Although I had requested the spotlight several months in advance of the conference, nothing had been done. I went to the office of the supervisor to arrange for the equipment and a person to run it. As I began talking to the supervisor, however, it was apparent that he felt under pressure because of other demands on him and that I would likely get nowhere by pushing my requests. Instead, I spent the next fifteen minutes listening—essentially assuming the role of counselor rather than that of negotiator. The second part of the conversation returned to my problem and some friendly negotiation to get the problem solved. The original conversation lasted about twenty minutes and is presented here condensed.

Supervisor: I don't know if I can do anything for you or not. I shouldn't even be here according to my doctor. I've got a doctor's appointment for one o'clock, so I won't be here this afternoon.

Visitor: Uhhuh. You'll be gone. [Reflecting—drawing implications.]

Supervisor: I have an assistant and I don't know when he'll be here. He had to work till after midnight last night. They should never hold a conference like this here. We don't have the facilities or the manpower. Everyone yells at me when I can't perform miracles.

Visitor: You haven't got enough help—that's the problem for this afternoon. Your assistant may be here. [Reflecting content—focusing on specifics related to visitor's own problem.]

Supervisor: Well, he's a student and only works part time. I just don't have any help. I've got a bleeding ulcer from this job and if I would follow my doctor's orders I wouldn't be here now.

Visitor: That sounds serious. [Reflecting—drawing implications.]

Supervisor: There's too much pressure. I'm responsible for far more than I can possibly do. Then if things aren't right, I'm the one who gets yelled at.

Visitor: Uhhuh. I see what you mean. And I come in and ask for one more thing. [Reflecting—summarizing siutation.]

Supervisor: It's not you. This job, they're always complaining about something.

Visitor: Uhhuh. [Nonverbal cues—listening noises.]

The conversation went on for some time with the supervisor telling me about his job and the pressure involved. He was the low man on the totem pole so he was catching a lot of flack which other people should have gotten. In addition, he was understaffed. The second part of the conversation proceeded as follows:

Supervisor: If other people weren't always borrowing the chairs from one room to put somewhere else this wouldn't happen. So, anyway, you need a spot and we've got one, but I don't have anyone to run it, unless my assistant can do it when he comes in.

Visitor: I really need the spotlight. . . . [I–statement stating wants] and I'm willing to run the equipment myself if necessary. [I-statement saying what he is willing to do.]

Supervisor: Well, I don't know. I could show you the equipment and when my assistant comes he can let you in later with his key, though he may not be here because he worked until after midnight last night and I don't know where he is.

Visitor: I see. You'll show me the spot and how to work it. That will be good. I'll still need to be able to get the light booth unlocked.

Supervisor: Well, as I say, I don't know when my assistant will be here and I'm leaving for the doctor as soon as I can get out of here.

Visitor: Yes, I realize that. [Focusing on an area of agreement.] Can you leave the keys with someone and I can pick them up?

Supervisor: (Wanting to solve the problem and leave) I'll just show you the lights and give you the keys. Just make sure you get them back to my assistant when he gets here or I'll be in trouble. Sure. That should take care of it. I really appreciate your helping me out.

We then went up to the light booth where I learned how to operate the equipment. After he showed me what I needed to know, he locked the door, gave me the keys and left. I had never met this man before and he didn't know me, yet after twenty minutes of telling me his life history, he took another twenty minutes to set me up, gave me his keys, and disappeared for the day. While I was listening I had no idea how or whether things would work out; I was listening to someone in distress. The fact that I listened and understood his problems, however, made a great difference in his attitude toward me and my requests. Also, as a result of listening I changed my request to fit the circumstances.

Solving the problems of others and solving one's own problems often occur together. Even in situations where your job is primarily that of meeting the needs of others, there is a need for you to meet your own needs. In situations where you are most concerned with meeting your own needs, helping others meet their needs is often the best way to create cooperation.

The second example illustrates many of the techniques involved in helping someone think through a problem and make a decision. The problem at hand was a simple one: Janice, a competent, professional woman in her forties with a husband and children of her own, was allowing herself to be manipulated by her mother into making daily phone calls which she did not like to make but which she felt guilty about not making. The comments in brackets identify the skills being used. The subheadings divide the conversation into sections identifying steps in the problem-solving process.

Identifying Specifics of the Problem

Janice: I'm tired of calling my parents every day, but if I don't, she calls me and makes me feel guilty.

Getting a Value Judgment

Leader: What do you think would be a reasonable number of times to call her each week? [Asking for specifics—focusing on responsibility for making decisions.]

Janice: Oh, every other day (mild laughter from group) . . . but I couldn't do it.

Leader: What's the worst possible thing that could happen if you didn't call? [Asking for specifics—focusing on worst possible consequences.]

Janice: My mother would call and make me feel guilty.

Leader: You wouldn't like it but would that be terrible and awful? [Asking for specifics—challenging worst possible consequences.]

Janice: It isn't, I suppose.

Leader: You don't sound convinced. [Reflecting client's tone of voice.]

Janice: Well, they're getting old and I feel I really should call them often. I don't know how long they'll be around.

Leader: As it is, though, you don't enjoy the conversations.

Janice: That's right. I feel I have to talk to them, whether I want to or not.

Leader: You feel compelled . . . [Reflecting feelings.]

Janice: I feel I have to.

6 / Introduction

Leader: What is there about the situation that makes you feel you *have to* call? [Asking for specifics.]
Janice: Nothing.
Leader: Well . . . what do you tell yourself? [Asking for specifics.]
Janice: Right. I'm telling myself I ought to.

Generating Alternatives

Leader: So what can you do about it? [Asking for specifics.]
Janice: Not call!

Asking for a Decision

Leader: Will you do that?
Janice: I won't call more than every other day.
Leader: We'll see what happens

Initially Janice saw the situation as a problem of changing her parents. She returned the next week and informed the group that she had called only once, hadn't felt guilty, and, more important, felt good about the call she did make.

Learning the Skills

There are several things you can do to get the most from this book. *First*, read in small chunks. This will give you time to think about what you have read, and to carry out two additional suggestions. *Second*, observe to what extent and in what situations the statements made in this book apply to you. All communication techniques are context bound, that is, they will work in many situations, but not in every situation. Observing your own behavior and that of others is crucial for learning the techniques. *Third*, in order to learn the techniques, practice them—at first in neutral situations so that you can acquire skill, later in more difficult situations. Chapter 18 contains suggestions for practicing the techniques, and you may find it useful to refer to it periodically as you prepare to try out the various techniques.

part one

CHANGING "HELPFUL" RESPONSES TO EFFECTIVE RESPONSES

If you have been practicing a skill for twenty years or more—let's say it's tennis—when you go to an expert, you want help in identifying and correcting what you are not doing well. You don't simply want to learn new skills, you want to *replace* ineffective actions with effective ones. So it is with the skills in this book—their effectiveness comes not from simply learning and using them, but from using them to replace ineffective behavior. Examining your own behavior and identifying areas in which you are not effective is a positive and important step for change. Learning a new technique in isolation makes it too easy to incorporate an otherwise effective technique into an ineffective style, with the result that the technique doesn't work.

Identifying ineffective behavior is encouraging in the long run because once you identify what is ineffective you can work to change it. The next two chapters examine ten patterns of communication which tend to produce defensive, image-centered interactions. By *image-centered* I mean any communication—verbal or nonverbal—that encourages people to compare themselves or others or the world to an idealized image (Martin, 1979a). When communication encourages people to focus on their image of self (self-image), they self-consciously defend themselves instead of thinking about what they can do to solve their problems.

The ten patterns we will examine are:

1. *Image-centered criticism:* Criticizing the person instead of focusing on specifics of the problem.

2. *Image-centered praise:* Positive evaluations aimed at changing the person instead of solving the problem.

3. *Guilt induction:* Communication that encourages guilt feelings.

4. *Reassurance:* Messages that insist that everything is O.K. when the person being reassured doesn't feel that they will be.

5. *Advice:* Messages that tell people what to do when they need to think through their own problems.

6. *Positive thinking:* Telling people their problems will be solved if they think positively.

7. *Sympathizing:* Telling others how bad you feel or how sorry you are about their problems.

8. *Logical argument:* Trying to persuade others to accept a particular solution instead of helping them think the problem through.

9. *Teaching, demonstrating, giving instructions:* Telling others how to do things before they want help.

10. *Questioning:* Asking questions, especially questions that put others on the defensive.

These ten patterns are seen as ways of influencing others. The purpose of the next two chapters is to show how and why these approaches do not work, or at best do not work as well as the alternatives (see Rogers 1942, Gordon, 1974, Bolton, 1979).

Learning to recognize these patterns in your own behavior allows you to either avoid them altogether (difficult but possible) or to consciously work on replacing them with the skills you will learn in Part II. The patterns we use

10 / CHANGING "HELPFUL" RESPONSES TO EFFECTIVE RESPONSES

are patterns we learned from our parents, teachers, peers, friends, and others. We didn't invent these patterns, we acquired them without being aware of them. When we become aware of the way in which we use language (and are used *by* language), we have new choices.

In observing your own behavior it is useful to take a positive attitude when you recognize your own ineffective behavior. Telling yourself, "That wasn't very effective, how could I handle that better next time?" is much better than, "Isn't it terrible I did that." Focus not on yourself, but on specific changes you can make. Learning to recognize these patterns is also useful when others are using these approaches on you. When you recognize these approaches you can avoid being manipulated and losing your own power to act. This is particularly important in situations in which you are expected to respond rationally no matter what the other person says. Further on, Parts Two and Three show how to develop the alternatives presented in Part One into five skills and five strategies for using the skills.

chapter one

Focusing on the problem (instead of the person)

Working effectively with people involves influencing people to change. Three common methods of trying to change people are *criticizing, praising,* and *inducing guilt feelings.* These ways of trying to influence people are attempts to change the person instead of to solve the problem. They work poorly because it is easier for people to change what they *do* than to change what they *are.* Attempts to change what people *are* discourages them and frequently leads to conflict. Encouraging others to change what they *do* is much more likely to be successful. Helping others to focus on problems and on what they can do about them removes the coercion and pressure from relationships, making them more personal and satisfying.

IMAGE-CENTERED CRITICISM: MISTAKEN FOCUS ON THE PERSON

Most criticism mistakenly focuses on the person instead of the problem. Working with other people requires zeroing in on problems quickly and efficiently without evoking defensiveness and self-consciousness. Criticism that results in people's feeling self-conscious and acting defensive gets in the way of solving problems. The approach developed by Albert Ellis (1979) and based on the work of Korzybsky (1933), a linguist, is very specific about what criticisms result in a mistaken focus on the person instead of the problem. This approach can be summarized in three statements:

- Where you would ordinarily say that someone *is* lazy, irresponsible, untrustworthy, and so on, substitute another verb and your sentence will be more specific and more problem-centered.
- Where you would ordinarily say that someone *always*, or *never* does something, substitute a more accurate estimate of the frequency with which a problem has been occurring.
- Where you would ordinarily say that someone *should*, *must*, *has to*, or *ought to* do something, say what the other person *could*, *might*, or *needs* to do in order to solve a particular problem.

Small changes in phrasing may seem unimportant, but details are what influence people to defend themselves instead of solve problems. We will examine these three patterns in more detail.

The Verb To Be

One way of labeling people is telling them what they *are* rather than what they *do*. Image-centered language often equates an individual, a group, a behavior, with a label such as *irresponsible, worthless, idiot, failure*, and so on:

Statement: You *are* irresponsible.

Message: You have not simply acted in an irresponsible way; as a person you are in essence irresponsible; you are irresponsible by nature and cannot change. At the same time, I expect you to start acting responsibly.

Sentences using the verb to be identify subject with predicate as if they share the same essence. So, for example, labeling someone as "irresponsible" identifies that person as being *in essence* irresponsible, incapable of being anything else. At the same time, the sentence implies that the individual *should* be different, *should* change.

Substituting another verb makes the sentence more specific (and usually more problem-centered). For example:

You didn't call and let me know you would be late.

You can also program yourself to act in self-defeating ways by using sentences such as (Ellis 1975, Ellis 1978, Ellis and Harper, 1975):

Statement: I *am* a failure.
Message: I am in essence a failure; I cannot be anything else. I cannot succeed, yet I should; I ought to and have to change.

This message may not be intended, but it is implied by the structure of the sentence. Such messages produce frustration and self-defeating patterns of behavior.

Eliminating the verb to be and substituting another verb results in a more specific statement, and more specific statements are usually more problem-centered and less image-centered. The sentence "I am a failure" might become any of the following:

- I failed the driving test.
- I didn't do as well as I would have liked.
- I made a mistake.

These statements are still self-critical, but they are now concerned with behavior and behavior can be changed.

Absolutes

Another way we focus on the person instead of the problem is by using absolutes such as *always, never, ever,* and *forever* to identify a person or a situation with a label:

- How come you are *always* in trouble?
- You are *never* on time.
- She is *forever* wasting time.
- They were *always* so irresponsible.
- Will you *ever* be happy?

These sentences are accusations. When you use absolutes, you are no longer talking about a specific situation, but a general or eternal condition. If you are frustrated when someone arrives late, you may be tempted to dramatize your frustration by exaggerating with a statement like: "You are always late!" Such sentences may be dramatic but they direct attention away from the problem of the other person's being late and focus on the person as being *always* a certain way.

Naming specific times or places or incidents requires you to become more problem-centered and is more likely to result in discussion of the problem. For example:

- What did you do that has gotten you in trouble?
- You have been late several times this week.
- She has been spending too much time around the water cooler lately.
- He acted irresponsibly when he didn't call and let you know he had an accident.
- What could you do to feel happier about your present situation?

These sentences are more specific and more problem-centered than the examples that contained absolutes.

Should, Would, Must, Ought To, and Have To

One of the most common ways of focusing on the person instead of the problem is telling others what they *should, would, must, ought to,* and *have to* do:

Statement: You *should* do your work better.
Message: You do not do your work well now and there is obviously something wrong with you or you would do better.

Another example:

Statement: If only you *would* stop drinking.
Message: You would be more worthwhile than you are now if you stopped drinking.

A third example:

Statement: You *must* do a better job.
Message: Better than you are doing now!

All of these statements compare *what is* to an ideal, they change the focus from what exists and what can be changed to what is fantasy. These comparisons imply a judgment of the person. In a mistaken attempt to produce a change in behavior, the speaker focuses on the person, implying that the individual is unworthy or unsatisfactory as a person. Far from encouraging change, such comparisons result in discouragement and defensiveness. By being specific about a problem, while eliminating the *shoulds*, *woulds*, *musts*, and *oughts*, you are more likely to focus on the problem.

Changing the three foregoing examples to eliminate image-centered words results in more problem-centered statements:

- Mistakes you are making in filling orders are causing a problem in the shipping department. I'd like to work out some procedures for double checking orders before you send them on.
- I'm concerned about the effect of your drinking on your relationships with your family and your colleagues.
- Your presentations give the impression that you haven't prepared and I'm concerned.

These are still confrontive statements, but they are more specific and more problem-centered. Chapter Six goes into more detail on confrontive I-statements and Chapters Twelve and Thirteen present two strategies for being problem-centered when you need to confront others without creating a conflict.

IMAGE-CENTERED PRAISE: MISTAKEN FOCUS ON POSITIVE EVALUATION

Praise is often presented as a positive way to get results. However when praise results in a focus on the person rather than on the accomplishment, it may be experienced as a threat. Praise that focuses on what people *are* rather than what they *do* tends to be ineffective. Praise that focuses on what people *do* is more likely to motivate and encourage.

The Message of Image-centered Praise

When we recognize that someone has a low self-opinion, it may be tempting to try to build up that person's self-image by using praise. However praise seldom convinces others that they are worthwhile, interesting, skillful, beauti-

16 / CHANGING "HELPFUL" RESPONSES TO EFFECTIVE RESPONSES

ful, or intelligent:

Manager: (Feeling discouraged.) I feel like a failure!
Friend: But you're a great manager! . . . .
Manager: Yes but . . .

Praise is a judgment—a positive judgment, but still a judgment, and a positive judgment implies the possibility of a negative judgment.

Trying to build a positive self-image by praising the other person identifies that person with a label. For example:

Statement: You are talented.
Message: Your talent is part of your essence, therefore you have no excuse for not producing. Your talent is always there, so your performance should always reflect that talent.

If the other person identifies with your label (that is, talented), then the loss of that label (for example, your performance causes me to question your talent), is a threat to that person's identity. Of course not everyone will react defensively to this type of praise, but when you are talking with someone who does react defensively, more specific, performance-oriented comments are more likely to be appreciated. For example, "You are talented" could become, depending on the circumstances:

- Your solution will help us do a better job.
- I enjoyed your performance this evening.
- Your time set a school record.

A general statement could mean anything. Focusing on specifics makes comments more immediate and potent.

A second example:

Statement: You are an excellent teacher.
Message: Since you *are* an excellent teacher, you should always behave as one; you have no excuse for not being excellent all the time and in every way.

More specific, performance-oriented comments would be:

- My son has enjoyed having you in class.
- I appreciate your enthusiasm and thoroughness.
- You handled a difficult situation very professionally.

In addition to creating less defensiveness, specific comments show that you understand and appreciate what is involved in the other person's accomplishments.

A third example:

Statement: You are beautiful.

Message: Your beauty should be unchanging; you have no right to feel that you are not beautiful; you have no right to think that you are not beautiful.

This is a glorious sentence, especially if it expresses your deepest feelings and if the other person can accept it as a statement of your feelings. On the other hand, such a statement made to a person who does not feel beautiful is likely to evoke disagreement ("No, I'm not!"). In such situations, more specific comments are more likely to be graciously received:

- I like your dress.
- I enjoy being with you.
- That shade of blue really suits you.

If the people you praise already feel good about themselves then your praise may encourage them. When you praise to convince others that they are worthwhile and they do not feel good about themselves, you are unlikely to succeed.

People tend to reject praise that contradicts their self-image:

A: I can't do a thing right! I just ruin everything I try to do!

B: Nonsense, you're an excellent student! [Mistaken attempt to build self-image by using praise.]

B's statements discounts *A*'s feelings. It implies that *A* has no right to these feelings. Finally, it discourages an honest look at the situation and what can be done about it. Praise of any sort is likely to be inappropriate in this situation. A better response would be to reflect *A*'s feelings ("You're upset about something you did...") or to ask for specifics ("What is it you didn't do right?"). Chapters Three and Five discuss these skills in detail.

Contradicting an individual's self-image invites an argument which the other person can always choose to win. Praise can encourage others, but it can also leave them feeling misunderstood:

Speaker: I'm not sure I can handle this new responsibility....
Listener: Your work has always been excellent and you're a very competent person. You won't have any trouble.... [Inappropriate praise.]

The listener may think he is encouraging, but how does the speaker feel? The listener's comments may be experienced as: (1) unwillingness to listen, (2) inability of the listener to understand his feelings, (3) additional pressure to do well. A more appropriate response is to listen and reflect (see Chapter Three) the speaker's concerns:

You're not sure you can handle the responsibility....

This response, followed by nonverbal encouragement (see Chapter Four), is much more likely to encourage honest discussion.

Another example:

Speaker: Things are just terrible. Everybody is mad at me because I'm doing better than they are. I had the highest rating in my group.
Listener: Well, that's great that you're doing so well—you should be glad. If the others are jealous that's their problem! [Inappropriate praise.]
Speaker: Well, I care if people won't talk to me anymore! [Angry about having concerns ignored.]

The listener, in an attempt to be encouraging, ignores the speaker's real concerns. Reflecting the speaker's concerns lets the listener encourage the speaker:

You're upset and it has to do with the high rating you got in your group.

Guidelines for Changing Image-centered Praise

Like image-centered criticism, changing image-centered praise involves making changes in three language patterns:

1. Where you would ordinarily use sentences that say that someone *is* beautiful, talented, efficient, a hard worker, successful, enterprising, and so on, use another verb and the sentence will be more specific.
2. Where you would ordinarily say that someone *always* or *never* does something, substitute a more realistic estimate of the frequency of that behavior.
3. Where you would ordinarily say that someone *should*, *must*, *has to*, or *ought to* be happy, think positively, act confidently, and so on, substitute the verb that suggests the possibility of a particular action as a solution (for example, the verbs *could*, *might*, or *it would be preferable if* . . . emphasize alternatives instead of the person).

These suggestions come down to focusing on specific behaviors or achievements when you think that praise is appropriate.

In situations in which praise is not appropriate, you may want to simply listen, using the skills of reflecting (Chapter Three) and responding nonverbally (Chapter Four). In some situations, expressing your appreciation may be more appropriate than giving praise (see "Expressing Appreciation" in Chapter Six).

INDUCING GUILT FEELINGS: MISTAKEN FOCUS ON BLAME AND GUILT

Like image-centered criticism and praise, inducing guilt feelings focuses on the person rather than the problem. Inducing guilt feelings is an attempt to change others by convincing them that they are worthless and must feel miserable until they change their behavior (Ellis 1975, 1977). Unfortunately guilt induction usually works in reverse; the more guilty people feel, the more paralyzed they become. Whatever short-term advantage you may gain, evoking guilt feelings reinforces powerlessness and irresponsibility. People will change only when they stop feeling guilty and focus on what they can do (Martin, 1979c, Dreikurs, 1967).

When people say they "feel guilty" they are usually referring to an internal state that combines feeling miserable and depressed with thoughts and images of being worthless, no good, inferior, and inadequate. By understanding how guilt feelings are induced, you can better (1) avoid guilt induction as a way of trying to help others, (2) avoid manipulation by others, and (3) help others cope with guilt feelings that interfere with their attempts to cope with problems.

Blaming and Nagging

Blaming and nagging are often delivered in a way that suggests: "You are not worthwhile unless you comply with my wishes."

Appeals to Caring

Messages such as the following put people in a position in which they feel they can't win:

- "Don't you care what people think?"
- "Don't you care about me?"
- "What will the neighbors think?"

The message communicated by such sentences is: either you do what I say, or you don't care (and should feel guilty). The person who says, "Yes, I care!" may feel obliged to give in. The person who says, "No, I don't care!" often feels guilty and ends up giving in anyway. The alternative is to realize that it is possible to care and to avoid giving in by saying, "I do care and I am going to do what I think is right."

Appeals to Love or Loyalty

Appeals to love ("If you really loved me, you would . . .") typically occur in male-female relationships and in parent-child relationships.

The apotheosis of the demand "If you love me . . ." is found in fairy tales where a male must prove his worthiness by slaying a dragon, climbing a glass mountain, or performing other tasks equally difficult and equally unrelated to love. Love is devalued by making it into a reward (e.g., the princess is always a reward—along with real estate, usually half the kingdom).

People don't prove their love by allowing themselves to be manipulated into feeling guilty. Likewise, they don't have proof of another's love because they manipulate that person into honoring their appeals. Appeals to loyalty function in much the same way.

Accepting Responsibility Instead of Feeling Guilty

In Part Four we will examine the problem of responsibility in detail, but a few words on the relationship of responsibility to guilt feelings are appropriate here. *Guilt* in the legal sense refers to responsibility for behavior. However *guilt feelings* are feelings of misery, fear, and dread accompanied by self-blame. As Ellis points out (1977), accepting responsibility (guilt in the legal sense) does not imply or require accepting blame and feeling guilty.

Accepting responsibility for one's own behavior is essential for changing and solving problems. Many people, however, confuse accepting responsibility with accepting blame and feeling guilty. Naturally they resist accepting responsibility. To avoid inducing guilt feelings in others, focus on the specifics of the problem or situation you want to discuss. Parts Two and Three show how to be specific without inducing guilt.

SUMMARY

Image-centered language:

- Reinforces a negative and self-defeating image. People who feel discouraged are especially likely to accept image-centered language at face value.
- Encourages powerlessness. A person who accepts image-centered language feels powerless to change.
- Paralyzes individuals so they can no longer find the courage to make decisions and take action.
- Reinforces resentment, self-hatred, and guilt feelings.

Image-centered criticism, image-centered praise, and guilt induction are common but ineffective approaches to changing others. Each of these methods focuses on trying to change the person rather than solve the problem. An alternative is to focus on the specifics of the problem when giving criticism and to focus on the specifics of the accomplishment when giving praise. When neither criticism nor praise is appropriate, the skills and strategies in Parts Two and Three present additional alternatives. In the next chapter we will look at seven other common but ineffective approaches to helping others.

chapter two

Changing seven "helpful" responses that don't work

When confronted with a problem situation, we tend to use the following approaches:

- Reassurance
- Advice
- Positive thinking
- Sympathy
- Logical argument
- Teaching, demonstrating and giving instructions
- Questioning

Although these approaches can be effective, in problem situations they tend to put others on the defensive. As with image-centered praise, criticism, and guilt induction, they generate resistance when they focus on the person instead of the problem.

REASSURANCE: WILL EVERYTHING REALLY BE O.K.?

To reassure means to instill confidence, and confidence is highly desirable in problem situations. Unfortunately much of what passes for reassurance does not instill confidence. Consider the following example:

Speaker: I don't know what to do. I'm really afraid of losing my job the way things are going with the economy and all. . . .
Response: Oh, it will be all right. Everything will be fine. [Inappropriate reassurance.]

How would you feel if you were the speaker? Probably not very reassured. The response denies the validity of the speaker's feelings (worry, frustration), the validity of the speaker's perceptions (likely job layoff) and closes off further discussion (what more can the speaker say if "everything will be fine"?). The response declares that there is no problem.

Typical phrases used to reassure include:

- Oh, it will be all right.
- Don't worry, things will be O.K.
- There, there, it's not so bad.
- Of course I still love you.
- I know you can do it if you just try.
- Everything will be fine, you wait.

Such reassurances seldom reassure (that is, instill confidence). They are more likely to elicit the following (usually unspoken) responses:

- You don't understand how I feel.
- You are trying to get rid of me.
- You aren't making me feel any better.

If you are upset you don't want someone telling you that everything is O.K., implying that you shouldn't feel upset. The fact is that you *do* feel upset, and you would like others to at least recognize the fact. When reassurance is given in a way that denies the other person's feelings, that person is likely to feel misunderstood and resentful. If you are experiencing your world falling apart you don't want to be told that your world isn't falling apart.

Genuine reassurance comes from listening to the other person, from taking the other person's feelings seriously, and by expressing your own concerns for the other person. The skills of reflecting (Chapter Three) and responding nonverbally (Chapter Four) are particularly effective in being an empathetic listener. I-statements (Chapter Six) are often appropriate for expressing concern.

GIVING ADVICE: MISTAKEN FOCUS ON TELLING OTHERS WHAT TO DO

Giving advice that provides information needed to make a decision can be an effective way of working with others. On the other hand, advice that attempts to solve the problems of others by making their decisions for them rarely helps and is often resented.

Stereotyped advice-giving is often a reflex. Eliminating sentences that begin with the following phrases is useful in avoiding giving advice:

- If I were you . . .
- Why don't you . . .
- Maybe you should . . .
- Have you ever thought about . . .
- Let me tell you what I would do . . .

Many of these sentences are deferential in tone, but they almost always end with suggestions that are far from deferential.

When someone specifically asks you for advice and you don't want to give it, you can truthfully tell the other person that you don't know what he or she should do. For example:

Question: Should I get a divorce?
Possible Answers: I don't know.
I'm not you, so I really can't say what I would do.
I wouldn't feel comfortable giving advice about this.

This need not be the end of the dialogue; it is just refusing to move in a nonproductive direction. Another approach is to use reflecting (Chapter Three) to keep the focus on the other person rather than on you.

POSITIVE THINKING: MISTAKEN FOCUS ON WILLING AND WISHING

By *positive thinking* I mean efforts to convince others that they can succeed by willing or wishing themselves to succeed: "You can if you think you can." Encouraging others to make an effort can be important in motivating them, but at the same time, such an effort tends to fail when it is used in place of listening to others.

Needing Help: I'm not sure if I can succeed. I've never taken much responsibility before; now I may be taking more than I can handle.

Helper: Of course you can! I know you can do it; you just need to believe in yourself a little more. [Inappropriate positive-thinking.]

People who habitually tell others "you can do it!" are likely to give the impression that they don't listen. In many cases they don't listen because they already know what they're going to say.

When positive thinking delivers the message: "Do this and everything will be all right," avoid it. If the other person accepts your advice and everything is not all right, you will be blamed.

Encouraging others to attempt the impossible may result in disillusionment when someone attempts an unrealistic goal and then fails. Be especially careful with people who try for perfection and want you to agree that they can accomplish the impossible. Your agreement may encourage unrealistic and ultimately self-defeating ideas. You can encourage others more by helping them think through problems and follow through on their decisions. Strategies 2 and 3 (Chapters Ten and Eleven) are particularly useful in accomplishing this.

SYMPATHY: MISTAKEN FOCUS ON FEELING SORRY FOR OTHERS

What people mean by sympathy is often feeling sorry for someone rather than empathizing, that is, feeling *with* someone. Whether expressed in words or communicated through nonverbal cues, feeling sorry for others encourages them to feel powerless and inferior.

Feeling sorry for someone often communicates the following messages:

* I am better than you.
* My attempts to be nice to you are only a show.
* You are so different from me that I can't identify with you.
* You are weak and powerless and can't help yourself.
* Your situation is terrible and awful and I don't want to think about it.
* I feel uneasy with you and I don't know what to do.

People may accept these messages as proof that they are inferior and to be pitied and may begin to pity themselves and to feel inferior, thinking:

* I am not as good as others.
* I make other people uncomfortable.
* I am different from other people.
* Other people only pretend to be nice to me.
* I am weak and powerless.
* My problems are terrible and awful and I am to blame for them.

Even competent, capable people who, through no fault of their own, have serious problems, may experience self-blame, guilt and self-hatred after being confronted with a pattern of sympathy mixed with condescending pity. For example, Ted has been fired from his job in a drive to economize. His friends don't know how to handle the situation and feel uncomfortable:

Friend: Hi! How are things going?
Ted: Not too good. I've just been let go; business has been down.
Friend: Gee, what a bad break. That's terrible [Feeling uncomfortable; sympathizing.]
Ted: Right. Well, I am busy looking around.
Friend: Listen, I'd love to talk, but I've got to run. . . . Say, can I loan you a few bucks? [Condescending, sympathizing.]
Message Communicated: I feel really uncomfortable talking to you. Now that there's something wrong with you, I have no time for you; I want to get rid of you as quickly as possible and still be a nice guy about it.
How Ted Feels: There's something wrong with me. I feel even more rejected, helpless, and powerless.

Ted's self-blame and guilt would be irrational, but the more Ted runs into similar situations, the more difficulty he will have not feeling guilty and worthless. By listening and expressing concern without either offering solutions or acting uncomfortable, his friend could have demonstrated to Ted that he is concerned about Ted and still accepts him as a friend.

People who have problems do not want to be treated with pity. Most want a chance to help themselves, or at least to cope with their situation. Consider how you would react if you were out of a job, or your wife had just left you, or one of your children had gotten into trouble—whatever it is—you wouldn't want people to look at you in that funny way that communicates: "you are not like the rest of us." We have all experienced this feeling at one time or another, but it is easy to forget how sympathy and pity can generate such feelings. The following comments show how sympathy can be misused:

> When I read about this "helpful" but often misused response, I couldn't help but think of a personal experience that I know of in regards to giving sympathy. My husband and I know a young couple who absolutely delight in being sympathetic. I have often doubted their sincerity but I never really realized why they did it. This young couple (I'll call David and Karen) started in dairy farming about eight years ago when we also started. So did about three other couples that were about in our age group. Of the five, David and Karen and we are the only ones left. Each of these other couples had very traumatic financial disasters in their lives; of which resulted two bankruptcies, one wife in a mental institution and another one is now a "born again" minister. Through each one of these other couple's miseries David and Karen used sympathy as a means of making themselves so secure. It was their way of putting down the others while building up their own egos. I never could really place why I always felt so angry when Karen would bring up the other couples' bad situations with a "Isn't it just too bad." I often wondered when I would be next on her "hit list" of the sympathy dole. For that reason I never told her any personal or financial problems.*

Empathy can be expressed without pity in many ways: through listening, through expressing your concern, through sharing your own feelings. The skills of reflecting (Chapter Three), responding nonverbally (Chapter Four), and using I-statements (Chapter Six) are particularly appropriate.

*Example used with permission.

LOGICAL ARGUMENT: MISTAKEN FOCUS ON CONVINCING AND PERSUADING

Logic is a valuable tool for thinking through problems and making decisions. However, using logic can become a problem if you try to persuade others to accept your solution or decision as a *substitute* for helping them think through problems.

Using logical arguments to coerce others into decisions they don't agree with may backfire when others do not accept responsibility for carrying out those decisions. Such situations tend to arise when a person feels responsible for pushing a particular solution. An argument may be logically correct and yet be ineffective. In the following example, Pam's goal is to encourage Bill to accept responsibility for his own behavior, an important step in achieving a sense of control over what happens to him. Pam's method evokes resistance, even though what she says is true.

Bill: ... So that's how it is, and there is nothing I can do about it.
Pam: But there is! If you accept some responsibility for what happens to you, you have a chance to change the situation! [Using logic.]
Bill: But there is nothing I can do. (Avoiding solution by objecting.)
Pam: I know how you feel, but if you think like that, then you are bound not to come up with anything you can do to make the situation better [Inappropriate use of logical argument.]
Bill: But you don't understand!
Pam: Look at it this way, if you don't accept responsibility for your behavior, then you will always feel like a victim because you won't feel like you can change anything. If you accept responsibility for your behavior, then you can focus on what you might do to change your situation. [Inappropriate use of logical argument.]
Bill: I don't see what I can do about it and you won't tell me anything that will work. [Resisting helper's argument.]

Pam's logic makes sense, but in this situation, using logic is inappropriate. Pam's language suggests she isn't listening ("I know how you feel . . ."). Listening and empathizing with Bill's feelings is more likely to encourage Bill to calm down and then examine what he can do about his situation. Pam could do this by using any or all of the five skills presented in Part Two. There is no one right response:

Bill: ... So that's how it is, and there is nothing I can do about it.
Pam: You don't know what to do about it... [Reflecting.]

Alternatively:

Pam: Uh huh... Go on... (nods head encouragingly). [Responding nonverbally.]

A third alternative:

Pam: I'm willing to listen and help if I can. [I-statement.]

Alternative four:

Pam: What is it that's keeping you from doing something? [Asking for specifics.]

Alternative five:

Pam: Sometimes it does seem like there's nothing that can be done. [Focusing on an area of agreement.]

Of course an infinite number of alternative responses could be generated, but the important point is to avoid trying to convince or persuade others before they have had a chance to explain their own position.

TEACHING, DEMONSTRATING, GIVING INSTRUCTIONS: MISTAKEN FOCUS ON TELLING OTHERS HOW TO DO THINGS

When you see someone doing a job less effectively than you think it can be done, it can very difficult not to jump in and try to show the other person "how to do it right." This applies especially in situations where you already have responsibility for teaching or supervising others. Until you have been "hired" (that is, your help is requested either explicitly or implicitly), teaching, demonstrating, or giving instructions will probably be resented, and may lead to a power struggle:

Frustrated: I just can't seem to get this right!
Helper: Here, let me show you how to do it!
Frustrated: Well,... [Becomes more and more frustrated as helper shows proper way to do task. Feels resentful and acts noncooperatively.]
Helper: I can't help you if you won't cooperate!

Such conversations take place between supervisors and employees, parents and children, teachers and students, counselors and their clients. Asking others if they want help is one way to avoid this dilemma. A simple inquiry such as, "Would you like me to show you another way of doing that?" or "Would you like to know what you could do?" is an effective way to find out if you are hired. In addition, by giving the other person the choice of whether or not you say any more, you are more likely to get a positive response.

If help isn't wanted, the other person will resist and resent your efforts. Unless you have been "hired" *by the person you are attempting to help, you will not be effective.* The greater the sense of control others feel in a situation, the easier it is to teach, supervise, or instruct.

QUESTIONING: MISTAKEN FOCUS ON INTERROGATION

Too many questions put people on the defensive. Chapter Five discusses effective questioning techniques but even these techniques will create defensiveness if overused. Questions are ineffective when they:

- Take control away from the person being questioned.
- Put the questioner on a superior level—especially by blaming or inducing guilt feelings.
- Put the person questioned on the defensive—especially asking for explanations or justifications asking the person questioned to justify himself.
- Change the subject, with the result that important information is lost.

A person who wants to talk will often "test the water" by referring to a problem in an indirect way:

Patient: Nobody has been here to visit me today. [Wanting to talk; testing the listener.]
Listener: Won't your husband be coming when he gets off work? [Inappropriate questioning.]

The listener is steering the conversation to what she is thinking about rather than what concerns the patient. The conversation may continue pleasantly enough, but the patient is unlikely to say much about what she really thinks.

The listener has delivered a subtle but unmistakable message that she is not tuned in to what concerns the patient, and as a result, the patient is unlikely to say what is on her mind. Empathizing with the patient's concerns by reflecting ("No one has been here to see you so far today") is more likely to encourage her to talk openly.

Many conversations proceed pleasantly enough, but any talk of what really concerns the individuals involved is avoided. Eric Berne (1964, 1976) identified this level of conversation as a *pastime*—conversations we have to pass the time that we use to deliberately avoid topics of concern to either side. The point is not to avoid all questions, but to develop a sensitivity to the desire of others to talk without being questioned.

Problems are created not so much by questions as such, but by too many questions and questions that take control of the discussion away from the speaker or put him on the defensive. The skills of reflecting and responding nonverbally (the next two chapters) are often more effective than questioning when you want to encourage others to talk. Questions that help people clarify or expand on what they want to say can be essential in solving problems, and in Chapter Five we will look at how to do this by *asking for specifics*.

SUMMARY

The final test of effectiveness is the other person's reaction. There may be times when the seven approaches described in this chapter can be used without creating a problem. Most of the time, however, these approaches tend to produce defensive, self-conscious behavior. To the extent others focus on the problem rather than on defending themselves, you can encourage others to change.

part two

THE FIVE SKILLS

To communicate effectively you need simple but flexible techniques. Learning a technique for use in a specific situation easily leads to stereotyped behavior: you have only one or two ways to respond in a particular situation. On the other hand, learning dozens of separate techniques allows flexibility, but may create problems in remembering and choosing a technique, especially in difficult situations. A third, better way to acquire an easily remembered, flexible set of techniques is to learn a small number of basic patterns. Learning patterns gives you unlimited flexibility within a simple, unified, coherent framework.

Each of the next five chapters demonstrates one of five basic skills for helping, working with, and living with others. Each skill consists of a group of related techniques that fall into an easily remembered pattern. The five skills and the chapters that describe them are:

- Chapter Three. GIVING FEEDBACK BY REFLECTING: Giving feedback by paraphrasing, summarizing, repeating key words or phrases, and drawing implications.
- Chapter Four. RESPONDING NONVERBALLY: Using listening cues and attentive silence.

- Chapter Five. ASKING FOR SPECIFICS: Asking questions that get down to the specifics of a problem without putting others on the defensive.
- Chapter Six. MAKING I-STATEMENTS: Asking for what you want; saying what you think and feel; setting limits.
- Chapter Seven. FOCUSING ON AN AREA OF AGREEMENT: Avoiding power struggles by agreeing in part, stating facts without contradicting, and admitting mistakes without being defensive.

These skills provide five alternatives for responding in any situation—considerably more than most people feel we have available at any one time. When you use these skills you also enable others to choose from more alternatives in thinking about and acting on their own problems.

chapter three

Skill one: Giving feedback by reflecting

Listening is an essential skill in developing any relationship. Listening not in the usual sense of hearing the other person's words, but in the sense of being able to enter into the other person's world and to reflect that world back to the speaker (Rogers, 1942, 1951). Reflecting, more than any of the skills we will examine, can communicate to others that you are listening and understanding. The skill of reflecting can also help you to listen more accurately, and without judging or distorting.

When you use reflecting you don't have to think about what you're going to say while the other person is talking because you base your response directly on what the other person communicates by words, gestures, or tone of voice. This is important because effective communication is based on giving your full attention to the other person.

Although reflecting is sometimes misunderstood to mean parroting what others have said, reflecting goes far beyond repetition.

Basic Principle

> Reflecting is an attempt to understand the total message—words, gestures, tone of voice, body language—and then to put that message into words.

We will look at four techniques for reflecting:

- Paraphrasing
- Summarizing
- Drawing implications
- Literal repetition

You do not need to think of these techniques as separate skills, but discussing them separately is useful in understanding reflecting.

PARAPHRASING

Paraphrasing allows you to reflect your understanding of a message in your own words (Brammer, 1973; Ivey & Authier, 1978). We do this spontaneously when we paraphrase directions or instructions to make certain we have understood correctly:

Motorist: How do I get to Kokomo from here?
Native: Turn left at the next light and follow Route 26 for about thirty miles till you see the signs for the turnoff to Kokomo—it will be a left.
Motorist: Let me see if I've got this straight. I turn left onto Route 26 at the next light, then turn left again about thirty miles down the road. [Paraphrasing.]

Paraphrasing to help others clarify their problems is an extension of this skill:

Teenager: When my mother got home, I didn't know what to do. The place was really a mess. We didn't mean to do anything—we were having a good time and things just got out of hand.
Listener: You made more of a mess than you meant to.... [Paraphrasing.]

Another example:

Ryan: I'm not sure if I can succeed. I've never taken this much responsibility before, and I may be taking on more than I can handle.
Kelley: You're not sure you can do the job.... [Paraphrasing.]

Effective paraphrasing requires close attention to the message. There are an unlimited number of ways to paraphrase, but not all paraphrases are going to be equally accurate in reflecting what the other person wants to say. The paraphrase should accurately restate what the other person has said in a simple and direct way. If you paraphrase everything you will sound like a parrot. Beginners often inadvertently call attention to themselves by trying to accurately restate everything the other person has just said. Instead of encouraging discussion, they end up inhibiting it.

SUMMARIZING

Especially when discussing a problem, people tend to digress, repeat, hesitate, or go over the same ground three times. *Summarizing* allows you to reflect a message in a concise way (Brammer, 1973; Ivey and Authier, 1978). Where continuous paraphrasing can become tedious and irritating, summarizing allows you to focus on a problem or concern without repeating or paraphrasing everything the other person has said:

Speaker: Yes, I'm thinking about when we should have our next meeting. I'm going to be out of town next Monday for our regularly scheduled meeting so we could meet later that week, or possibly just skip our meeting for that week entirely, ... there's not much point in meeting late in the week and then meeting the following Monday....

Listener: So ... we should have a meeting early that week or cancel until the week after. [Summarizing.]

The speaker is thinking through a problem aloud. Rather than making suggestions or giving advice, the listener enters into the process by helping to crystallize options.

Another example:

Speaker: My roommate is driving me crazy. I can't sleep at night because she stays out till late and then comes in making noise and turns on the lights and I can't get back to sleep. She's always got friends here when I want some peace and quiet or when I need to get something done.

Listener: Your roommate's coming in late is really causing a problem. [Summarizing.]

The listener summarizes the situation without taking sides. As a listener you don't have to agree with the other person's viewpoint in order to summarize that viewpoint.

DRAWING IMPLICATIONS

Drawing implications allows you to reflect a message not actually stated but nonetheless clearly implied. This can be important in clarifying a vague or confusing message. An example:

Client: Well, it just seems like my mother is always on my case. She wants me to go back and live with her and I suppose it would be a nice idea, but we would be fighting after the first day. She makes me feel guilty whenever I call; I just don't feel like calling her any more, yet I know I should. I don't see how going back and living with her would help anything. I love her and all, but . . .

Helper: You love her; at the same time you don't want to live with her. [Drawing implications.]

The client says she doesn't "see how going back and living with her [mother] would help anything." She avoids stating her true feelings: she doesn't want to go back home. By making this implication explicit, ("You love her; at the same time you don't want to live with her"), the helper says in a direct way what the client is saying indirectly.

At times drawing implications requires hypothesizing about the other person's message. The purpose is to help the other person discover what he is attempting to say, not to tell him what he means. Take care not to put words into the other person's mouth.

If the other person does not agree with your interpretation, don't insist on that interpretation. Making a mistake in interpretation seldom causes problems. Your mistake will often encourage the other person to clarify his position, provided you demonstrate your willingness to change your interpretation. Drawing implications often involves hypothesizing, but it should be simply an extension of the other reflective techniques and not a radical departure from them.

REPEATING KEY
WORDS AND PHRASES

Repeating important words and phrases allows you to reflect key elements of a message without having to put them into your own words. For example:

Speaker: Yeah, I want to get out of teaching . . . get a job in industry. I want to try something else, get another job, a chance to do something new. . . .

Listener: (Nodding head) ... another job ... [Repeating key phrase.]
Speaker: Yeah, I'm thinking about getting into audio-visual equipment and home computers. That's something I have experience with.

Just by these two words, "another job," and appropriate gestures, the listener encourages her friend to continue. These two words ("another job") seem to say nothing, but they communicate that the listener understands the speaker's concerns.

Another example:

Child: How can I go home now? My Dad's mad at me, my Mom's mad at me; no one wants to listen to me.
Listener: They're mad at you ... (nods head). [Repeating key phrase.]

Repeating a key word or phrase may seem the most simple of the reflective techniques, but it can effectively be used to accomplish the tasks of paraphrasing, summarizing, or drawing implications.

The most difficult part of using reflective techniques is overcoming the tendency to think about what you are going to say next. This tendency breaks one's concentration on what the other person is saying, often resulting in mismatched statements. Knowing that you can repeat a key word or phrase allows you to pay attention to the speaker without needing to think about your own reply. If you pay attention to the other person, you will almost always respond in a relevant way. On the other hand, if you pay attention to your own thoughts and to what you will say, you will tend to respond inappropriately.

DECIDING WHAT TO RESPOND TO

All reflecting involves choosing which message to reflect (Carkuff 1977, 1980; Carkhuff and Anthony, 1979; Egan 1975, 1976; Ivey and Authier, 1978). There are four types of messages that you could reflect in even the simplest communication:

Subject Matter: The more obvious content of the words.

Feelings: Emotional state of the speaker as well as attitudes about the message.

Nonverbal cues: Facial expression, body movement, tenseness (see Perls, 1969).

Hidden   Concerns that the speaker doesn't express directly, or even at-
Agendas: tempts to conceal.

Which message you reflect depends on a variety of factors. In the following situation a mother comes in to a psychologist to consult with him about her daughter, age nine, fourth grade, who is having trouble in school. The psychologist finds that the mother has several concerns:

Mother: (Looking worried) Ann isn't doing well in school. We just moved. My husband and I were separated for a while, but now we are back together and things are better. I hope you can help Ann. She's been in the hospital recently and she doesn't seem well enough to do everything the school is demanding....

In these few sentences the mother has communicated a substantial amount of information. The psychologist might respond to messages at any of the four levels, or to a combination of levels:

Reflecting   Ann isn't doing well in school.
Subject
Matter:

Reflecting   You are worried about Ann.
Feelings:

Reflecting   You look tense. This situation has been pretty hard on you.
Nonverbal
Cues:

Reflecting   You're possibly concerned about how your relationship with
Hidden   your husband is affecting Ann.
Agendas:

All four replies might be appropriate or none of them might be. How do you decide? In an actual situation we seldom decide what to say in a conscious, well-thought-out way. At that moment, thinking about all the possibilities is likely to create more problems than it solves.

It is useful to be aware of four factors in choosing a reply:

- The main message.
- What the other person wants.
- Your relationship with the other person.
- Your own thoughts and feelings.

We will consider each of these briefly.

The Main Message

Reflecting a speaker's main message is often the most appropriate response. This means reflecting the other person's main concern rather than reflecting what interests you. Reflecting something other than a main message may evoke a negative response. For example, in the situation we have just discussed, reflecting the mother's anxiety in a direct way ("You look anxious. . . ."), might be inappropriate. She might resent the psychologist for changing the focus from her main concern (her daughter's problem) to her anxiety. Be careful in referring to the other person's nonverbal behavior, even when it is the main message, as such references are likely to result in defensiveness. This brings us to the next consideration: What does the other person want?

What the Other Person Wants

Which message is appropriate to reflect depends in part on what the other person wants. You don't need to avoid reflecting a message only because the other person may not want to hear it. On the other hand, it is all too easy to use reflecting techniques to focus on what interests you instead of on the other person's concerns. This is using the reflecting techniques in a manipulative way. For example, if a mother is consulting me about her daughter, then that is what I have been hired to do. No matter how convinced I might be that this mother needs to talk about her own feelings before she talks about her daughter, if I have not been hired (either literally or figuratively) then I am in danger of imposing my perceptions on her if I call attention to her anxiety. In general, *be careful about referring explicitly to the other person's nonverbal behavior*. Referring to nonverbal behavior is sometimes frowned upon in our culture and others may react negatively. For example, telling a child he or she looks tired is a good way to invite an argument. On the other hand, reflecting nonverbal cues that accurately reflect another's feelings can be an effective way of encouraging the other person to talk.

Your Relationship with the Other Person

Are you speaking to the other person as a friend? A colleague? A member of the family? You can use the skill of reflecting regardless of whom you are talking with, but what is appropriate to reflect to one person may be inappropriate with another. Also, what is appropriate to reflect at one time may not be appropriate at another time with the same person. When you use reflecting, rely on your own sense of what you can say to a particular person. In teaching the skills, I have seen and heard about situations in which people have used reflecting (or any of the other skills) in an obviously inappropriate way. When I asked these people whether they thought their response made sense, they admit they didn't think so, but they thought they were using the technique, thinking that this meant they were to use a formula in a mindless way. The techniques have no magic in themselves. A reflecting response that is foreign to you or to the other person is probably not going to be understood or appreciated.

Your Own Thoughts and Feelings

Awareness of your own thoughts, feelings, and attitudes can be a valuable source of information about what is happening in an interaction. Your feelings can easily affect your response. If you ignore or are not aware of how you feel, you may say what you think is the "right" thing to say, but it comes out sounding wrong. This is particularly true of feelings of frustration, anger, or resentment. If you are aware of your feelings, you are less likely to attempt to rescue someone as a way of dealing with your own discomfort. The more aware you are of feelings of anger or resentment toward someone, the less likely you are to persecute that person when he or she doesn't seem to want to cooperate.

Personal needs and feelings can distort our attempts to help others when we aren't aware of them. When we aren't aware of our own feelings and attitudes, we may push a conversation in a way which meets our own needs rather than the needs of the person we're attempting to help. Being aware of your own feelings and attitudes allows you to take them into account in responding. For example, when I feel frustrated with someone who I think could do a better job, if I can become aware that I want to make this person act differently, I can usually avoid image-centered language. If I am not aware of wanting to change the other person, I am likely to use image-centered language in an effort to get immediate results. When this happens, I am not responding to what is happening at the moment; I am reacting on the basis of what I think should be happening.

When we are not aware of what we are thinking or feeling, we easily say and do things we later regret. Coercive, ineffective attempts to help often are a result of our image of what should happen. When things don't go as we think they should, we easily act in manipulative and coerceive ways.

When you become aware of what you are thinking and feeling you can change what you do. For example, if you don't notice that you are angry until after you say something angrily, you can't change what you've just said. If you notice yourself becoming angry, and are aware that you want to say something in an angry tone of voice, you can control your anger.

Letting Yourself Respond in the Situation

In an actual situation you can let yourself respond without deliberately choosing a response. We tend to think of choosing a response as a deliberate decision, but we often choose more effectively from moment to moment without making deliberate choices. In performing any skill (for example, driving a car, playing a musical instrument, typing a letter, playing football) we make moment-to-moment choices on the basis of our interaction with the task at hand. Communicating effectively is a skill. The more skill you have, the more you can focus on the needs of the situation, and the less you need to fumble around deliberately searching for a response.

APPROPRIATE USES OF REFLECTING

Helping Others Clarify Their Own Thinking

At times people speak not to explain or inform but to clarify their own thoughts. By reflecting your own understanding of a message, without interjecting your own opinion, you can help others clarify their own thoughts and feelings. We will look at dialogue examples of this in Part III, but a short example at this point may be helpful.

A young woman, supporting herself and living away from home, came in to my office upset by a phone call announcing that her older sister was planning to move in with her. The young woman wanted to be on good terms with her sister, but immediately realized that the two of them could not live together without constant friction. She saw no way out of the situation, feeling that whatever she decided there would be trouble. Her beliefs about family loyalty were in conflict with her feeling that allowing her sister to move in would result in an unworkable situation.

When I paraphrased, summarized, and drew implications from her conflicting messages, she was able to sort out what she wanted from what her sister wanted. Once she was able to sort out her confusion by putting it into words, she quickly came to a conclusion about what to do. She still felt uneasy, but she knew what she wanted. In one sense she already knew what she wanted to do before we talked, but her ideas about what a good sister *should* do became confused with her own needs, until she was able to put this conflict into words.

Clarifying Your Own Understanding of a Message

Reflecting allows you to find out whether you are correctly understanding what the other person is saying. An advantage of reflecting is that if you make a mistake in decoding a message, the other person will usually correct you without feeling attacked or threatened. Where judgmental statements or quesions may easily create conflict, reflecting encourages clarification.

Encouraging Others to Talk

Reflecting encourages others to talk, especially if they want to talk but feel hesitant. When people find you are willing to listen and enter into their point of view, they will tend to say what they think and feel.

Encouraging the Other Person to Direct the Flow of Communication

Reflecting allows the other person to direct the flow of the conversation. People who feel in control of a conversation are more likely to feel secure and, as a result, to say what they think. People who want help often feel defensive, powerless, or inferior. Questioning, advising, praising, and so on, tend to increase those feelings. Reflecting, on the other hand, gives the other person power to direct the flow of conversation, while giving you much more information than you are likely to get using traditional methods.

Changing Your Own Image-centered Responses

Using ineffective, image-centered language is often a well-established habit. *Reflecting* is an excellent substitute for image-centered language. The following comments were made by a woman who recognized a need to change her behavior, but didn't know how to change. Learning the reflecting skills gave her specific behavior to practice, which changed her relationships:

During the last few months, I've realized that I have the horrible habit of second-guessing and interrupting other people during conversations. This especially upsets me because they are two of the things that most infuriate me in other people. Not long ago, my husband was trying to tell me about what his day at work had been like. Every fourth word, there I was, finishing sentences (incorrectly, by the way), guessing outcomes, and interrupting—until he gave up and became quiet. I realized this too late and resolved to behave differently next time.

The next time he began to talk about work, I made a point of looking directly at him while he talked, rephrasing bits of what he was saying to let him know that I had heard him and to help me remember it. (I remember with embarrassment the time that he had just finished about ten sentences, of which I did not hear one, and then asked him about what he had just told me.) By listening, I enabled myself to give my husband my full attention, and I know by the way he acted and talked that he appreciated it. I'm trying to practice this more and more, and I can tell the difference it's making—he's talking a lot more and sharing more things with me. (Martin, 1980, p. 80.)

Avoiding the Trap of Mistaken Problem Ownership

Reflecting allows you to listen and empathize without accepting responsibility for solving another's problems. By contrast, questioning, judging, or otherwise manipulating and coercing others is actually a way of accepting responsibility for solving someone else's problem.

INAPPROPRIATE USES OF REFLECTING

Overusing

Beginners often use reflective listening responses which are either too long or which interrupt the flow of the discussion. A little reflecting goes a long way. When others are telling you their problems, let them do most of the talking. Reflecting responses may constitute less than ten percent of a conversation, and will encourage genuine dialogue.

Avoiding Dialogue

Reflecting can be used to avoid disclosing your own thoughts and feelings. People may resent you if you use reflecting to avoid making decisions, sharing your feelings, or saying what you think. (Chapter Six shows how to use I-statements to state your own thoughts and feelings.)

Distorting Messages

The easiest misuse of reflecting is distorting what the other person is saying. Paraphrasing, summarizing, drawing implications, or literally repeating what another person says is not sufficient for effective reflecting. Effective reflecting requires that you enter into the other person's reality.

SUMMARY

On a calm day, a pool of water is a perfect mirror reflecting sky, clouds, and surrounding landscape—everything that comes within its range. When the water is disturbed, its reflections become distorted or disappear altogether. People who simply listen, with no hidden agenda of their own, with nothing to gain or lose (no self-interest) can be a perfect mirror, reflecting without distorting. Listeners who are confused about what to say, who have their own axe to grind, or who judge others, distort what others say, or misunderstand altogether. Listening and reflecting are interrelated. Listening allows us to reflect accurately; reflecting encourages us to listen carefully.

Few communication skills have been more misunderstood than reflecting, yet few skills are more useful. The misunderstanding comes from the mistaken idea that reflecting means parroting what others say. The essence of reflecting is entering into the other person's way of seeing, hearing, feeling, and thinking. The techniques of paraphrasing, summarizing, repeating key words and phrases, and drawing implications are a means toward this end.

chapter four

Skill two: Responding nonverbally with attentive silence and listening cues

Speaker: (on the phone) I don't think I'm going to get together with you today. My father just had a heart attack and ... (pause)
Listener: Uh huh ... (concerned tone of voice, waiting for the caller to go on)
Speaker: (Says nothing; silence continues.)
Listener: (Encouragingly) Go on ...
Speaker: Well, I wanted to call and ... (speaker continues).

What do you say when the other person stops talking? Even a few seconds of silence may make you sufficiently uncomfortable that you feel compelled to start asking questions or talking. Four of the skills we will examine in this book are concerned with verbal replies; this chapter takes up the useful skill of responding nonverbally with attentive silence and listening cues. We use these responses spontaneously; by being more aware of their potential to encourage others to talk and to accept more responsibility for the conversation, we can use them more effectively.

ATTENTIVE SILENCE

Attentive silence indicates to others that you are listening and is a cue that prompts them to speak. Research (Mary Budd Rowe, 1974) shows that increasing the time you wait for others to respond to your questions will increase both the quantity and quality of their answers. Most people overestimate the length of silence in a conversation, perhaps because their perception is affected by their feeling of being under pressure.

You communicate attentiveness through eye contact, body posture, facial expression, and through gestures such as nodding (Hall, 1959; Knapp, 1980).

Encourage others to be relaxed and open by being relaxed yourself. People react to facial expression often without realizing that they are doing so. In particular, how relaxed your facial muscles are (as opposed to having tense muscles) can easily affect the other person's impression of your interest and willingness to listen. How well you reflect nonverbally the other person's expressions affects the degree of rapport you develop with the other person.

Others will talk more freely when they're relaxed than when they are literally "up tight." If you want other people to be relaxed and to express their thoughts and feelings you can encourage them by being relaxed yourself. If you are relaxed and attentive, your facial expression will tend to mirror your own interest, concern, and involvement with the other person's world. For example, if you are relaxed you will smile easily; on the other hand smiling is a way of relaxing—you can't smile without relaxing. I am not talking about smiling on cue or as a technique (the frozen smile) but as the external expression of an interior feeling of joy or pleasure or the recognition that something is funny or amusing or incongruous or ironic—whatever you find yourself wanting to smile at.

This relationship between internal feelings and external expression is illustrated by the limiting case—severe depression. A severely depressed person may avoid smiling as a way of avoiding feelings. Smiling means taking a risk—a small one—but a risk of feeling.

Maintain eye contact. Maintaining eye contact while the other person talks communicates that you are paying attention. If you look off into space while the other person talks you may communicate a message that what the other person says is unimportant or that you are not interested. Don't try to do something else while you are listening; put whatever you are working on aside and turn your full attention to the person you are talking with. However do not hold eye contact for a prolonged period of time (staring) as this may be interpreted as aggressiveness.

Sit or stand close enough to establish eye contact easily without invading the other person's personal space. (You will know if you have invaded another's personal space if he or she starts edging away.) In general, the closer (up to a point) two people are, the more willing they may be to say what they really think. This is obvious for two people of the opposite sex who have a close relationship, but it is also true that any two individuals who are seated facing each other over a low table are more likely to engage in more intimate conversation than two people who are seated six feet apart, with one person behind a huge desk. Even more interesting to me is the willingness of people to talk freely about personal concerns in front of a group of thirty or more, provided the people who conversing are close together and can establish eye contact readily.

If you want to establish a sense of contact with the other person, stand or sit close enough to establish eye contact easily (three to six feet) without invading the other person's personal space.

When you talk, you are assuming responsibility for the time you remain speaking. This is obvious, but the consequences are important: By remaining silent, you allow the other person to accept responsibility for speaking. A person who wants to say something important, but feels reluctant to do so, will sometimes wait, giving you a chance to interrupt. Your willingness to speak may rescue him from taking the risk of going on.
Example:

Speaker: What do you think I should do?
Listener: I don't know what you should do.... (Followed by silent waiting.)
Speaker: (continuing) I know you can't tell me; I'm just finding it hard to make a decision ... (etc.).

LISTENING CUES

There are times when it is useful to break silences without commenting or asking questions. We do this naturally by using words, grunts, and noises such as:

- Uh huh
- Mm hmm
- Yeah

- Oh
- I see
- Go on
- Continue
- Tell me more

These words and noises have no substantive content, but they let the other person know that we are listening, paying attention, and understanding (Gordon, 1974; Ivey and Authier, 1978).

The following group of words is also used to communicate interest and attention, but these words suggest an evaluation (however positive) and may easily be overused:

- Good
- Right
- O.K.
- Terrific
- Fantastic
- Great

All of these cues can be said in a variety of ways which match the other person's mood, tone of voice, and message.

As with all communication, *how you say something is as important as what you say*. Even a neutral cue like "Uh huh" can be used to suggest approval or disapproval, interest or lack of interest:

Young Child: I skipped school today! (Smiling slightly, good eye contact, subdued but enthusiastic tone of voice conveying the message: I'm sharing a secret with you.)

Listener: Uh huh... (Nodding head, matching child's voice tone, suggesting a willingness to share in the secret as a fellow conspirator.)

This approach may be very useful in encouraging a child who ordinarily won't talk to adults to be quite candid with an adult he has never even met before. Using the same listening cue with different nonverbal cues results in a different message:

Young Child: I skipped school today!

Listener: Uh huh... (Nodding head, slight irritation in tone of voice, communicating a sense of holding back, possibly of judging.)

In this situation the child may not pick up on the hint of irritation and go on with what he wants to say, or he may notice and respond with hesitation, uncertain about what to do next. A third example, same listening cue, different message:

Young
Child: I skipped school today!

Listener: Uh huh ... [Clipped, harsh tone of voice, staring at child, communicating a sense of disapproval.]

The message conveyed by a particular look, tone of voice, and wording cannot be easily pinned down. The other person reacts instinctively without being aware of the reaction.

Responding nonverbally is particularly useful in avoiding defensive behavior. A psychiatrist friend of mine who works with children and their parents is a master of this technique. By simply responding nonverbally as if what the client had said was in no way directed at him, he neatly deflates statements meant to shock, anger, or upset him. Here is a typical example:

Teenaged
Patient: You promised to be here at 4:00 and it's 5:30.

Psychiatrist: (Completing hospital rounds) Uh huh ... (Smiling, nodding head in good-natured agreement without acting defensive.)

Responding nonverbally is particularly useful in eliciting information—a skill which is valuable in business, particularly in management and in selling. In management, the more information you have about others, their attitudes, their problems, how they think, and so on, the more informed your plans and decisions will be. In selling, the more you find out about the other person's problems, wants, and needs, the more able you will be to make sales that are designed to meet customers' needs and solve their problems.

APPROPRIATE USES OF NONVERBAL RESPONSE

An Alternative to Talking

Responding nonverbally is a way of indicating attention without interrupting. If you tend to interrupt, using listening cues *instead* of talking is an excellent way to change your own behavior patterns.

Encouragement to Continue

Responding nonverbally encourages the other person to continue talking. Particularly when there is a pause in what the other person is saying, using listening cues leaves the responsibility for what is said next to the other person (Hackney and Nye, 1973). Being a good listener is not so much a matter of learning to listen, but of learning to not take responsibility for controlling or directing the conversation. This tendency is strongest when there is a pause, a silence in the conversation. It is difficult to avoid feeling uncomfortable in these (usually) brief periods of silence. The tendency is to improvise in these situations; to say whatever comes to mind. Unfortunately what often come to mind are comments or advice that interrupt or change the flow of the conversation.

WHY RESPONDING NONVERBALLY (INSTEAD OF TALKING) IS DIFFICULT

Sometimes we know it would be better to respond nonverbally but we have trouble following through. The difficulty is often a result of feelings of discomfort that are based on mistaken beliefs. By recognizing these beliefs and substituting more rational statements, you can reprogram yourself to feel and act more comfortable in responding nonverbally.

I Have to Keep Things Moving

You may feel you have to keep things moving if others expect you to have everything under control or if you expect yourself to have everything under control. The more you try to control others the more difficulty you are likely to have and the more uncomfortable others feel. The more we try to control things, the less well things seem to go.

Especially in a leadership role, it is easy to feel pressure to keep people talking and keep things moving. The more responsibility you take for keeping a discussion going, the less responsibility others are likely to feel for participating. And you end up responsible for silence. On the other hand, if you let silence happen without trying to avoid it or get rid of it, other people will tend to accept responsibility for speaking.

A more rational alternative to the thought "I have to keep things moving," would be: *I would like to keep things moving, but I don't have to accept all the responsibility.* Another rational alternative would be: *I want to say something and I find it difficult to wait, but I can wait.*

I Have Something Important to Say

It sometimes happens that, as someone else is speaking, we want to say something we think will be helpful. Instead of waiting for an appropriate time (if one should occur), we tend to stick in the comment at the first opportunity. When the feeling that you have to say something gets in the way of keeping silent, an alternative to interrupting is to tell yourself: *"I don't have to interrupt; I can say this later if it's still important."*

I Can't Stand the Silence

Some years ago in a group of graduate students, a woman in her early twenties was particularly upset because of the silences which developed in the group. She blamed me for not doing something about them. She was very set in the idea that I was wasting her time, and it took long discussion to get across the idea that her feeling upset was something that she was doing to herself, not something that others (or the silence) was doing to her. Marvelous comments, which would not otherwise have been said, came out of the silences, but she didn't notice. When silence developed, she would start thinking about all the things she needed to get done and daydream about them and feel anxious. No longer aware of what was going on, she felt bored and frustrated.

Difficulty in "standing the silence" is often related to our beliefs (what we tell ourselves). If you find it difficult to cope with silence, you may be telling yourself something like this:

- I'm wasting my time.
- I'm not getting anything done.
- I have more important things to do.

By believing such ideas you create an excuse, a rationale for not remaining silent. A more rational statement would be: *I find it difficult to stand the silence, but I don't have to talk.*

INAPPROPRIATE USES OF RESPONDING NONVERBALLY

Expression of Impatience

Occasionally you may respond nonverbally in ways that communicate impatience. Impatience will tend to evoke self-consciousness in the speaker, which further slows down or confuses the speaker.

Pretending Attention

People sometimes use nonverbal responses to fool others into thinking they are paying attention when they're not. An example is the stereotyped husband who sits reading a newspaper saying, "Uh huh" while his wife talks.

Pretending to pay attention communicates a double message: at one level the speaker picks up the message that he isn't being heard; at another level the speaker picks up the message that he is being heard. The speaker may not be aware of what is happening, yet feel uncomfortable or hostile.

SUMMARY

We encourage and orient one another as much through nonverbal means as through the words we use. Attentive silence encourages others to talk. Commonly used listening cues, such as "mmhmm...," also encourage others to talk. More important, attentive silence and listening cues leave the responsibility for the flow of the conversation to the other person.

Responding nonverbally is also an excellent way of resisting the pressure to say the first thing that comes to mind. The more we are aware of our own behavior, the better able we are to understand and change ineffective patterns.

Most of the techniques in this book have to do with responding verbally rather than nonverbally. In an actual conversation, however, silence and nonverbal responses are a large part of your responses as a listener. You are more likely to be ineffective by talking too much than too little. When we are talking we easily lose our awareness of how the other person is reacting. We miss a change in expression, tone of voice, posture, or wording, perhaps because we are thinking about what we're going to say, and we have lost contact with the other person.

Using silence and nonverbal skills allows you the space and the time to be aware of what is happening from moment to moment so that when you do speak, you are responding to what is happening at the time. The danger with all techniques is that they may become simply another routine. Using silence and nonverbal techniques won't *make* you more aware, but they will allow you to develop a greater awareness of the other person.

chapter five

Skill three: Asking for specifics

People have difficulty solving problems when they don't know how to zero in on specifics. We have already looked at one skill for staying problem-centered—reflecting. Reflecting can be very powerful, especially when others know what they want to say, where they want to go, and how they want to get there. When others are vague about their goals and alternatives, you may need to ask questions that encourage them to focus on the problem without becoming defensive (Hackney and Nye, 1973). Knowing how, when, and where to ask questions, and in particular knowing *what* questions to ask is often valuable in problem-solving situations. In this chapter we will look at questions that make it possible to establish a basis for action and then to choose a course of action. All of the questions we will examine will help you to get down to the specifics of what the problem is, what the alternatives are, and what people want to do.

Questions useful in *establishing a basis for action* include:

- What happened? [Focusing on the situation.]
- What did you do? [Focusing on actions.]
- How did (do) you feel about it? [Focusing on internal reaction.]
- What is that.... (feedback vague phrases)? [Requesting others to be specific in their criticism.]

Follow-up questions useful in pursuing relevant details include:

- Can you give an example? [Encouraging specifics.]
- Can you be more specific? [Encouraging specifics.]
- In what way? [Encouraging specifics.]

Once a basis for action has been established, you can ask questions aimed at *choosing a course of action*. These include questions on *value judgments*, on *consequences*, on *what the other person wants*, and on *plans and decisions*.

Questions on *value judgments* include:

- Is what you are doing making things better or worse?
- Is what you are doing helping?

Questions that focus on *consequences* include:

- What will happen if. . . . (fill in alternative)?
- What is likely to happen?
- What is the worst possible thing that could happen?

Questions that focus on *what others want* include:

- What do you want?
- What do you want to see (hear, feel)?

And finally, questions that focus on *making plans and decisions* include:

- What can you do about it?
- What are you going to do about it?

Most of these questions focus on "what."

Basic Principle

> *Invite problem-centered responses by asking "what?" rather than "why?"*

"Why?" puts people on the defensive by asking them to explain, to defend, to give reasons. "Why" questions invite rationalizations and excuses rather than discussion of problems.

Asking for specifics allows you to ask for the relevant specifics by paying attention to where you and the other person are in the process of problem-solving. The real beauty of the skill comes in realizing that, like using the skill of reflecting, if you pay attention to others, they will provide you with the cues and information you need to respond appropriately.

ESTABLISHING A BASIS FOR ACTION

In this section we will examine, one at a time, some of the questions useful in establishing a basis for action. In using this skill, at least at the beginning, I recommend you use the wording I have given, and then, after you have mastered the use of a particular question, to experiment with different wording.

What happened?

Ron: I can't believe it—I thought I had everything under control, and then the roof caved in!
Jan: You look pretty upset [reflecting], what happened? [Asking for specifics.]

People tend to describe problems in general terms, but they can see what might be done only by looking at specific details. By asking "what happened?" you can get the other person to focus on specific problems and you can spend more time actually exploring the problem.

What did you do?

Child: She hit me first!
Adult: What did you do?
Child: But she hit me first!
Adult: I hear you, but what did you do?

Asking, "What did you do?" without implying blame or judgment is important because people tend to avoid looking at their own behavior to avoid blame and guilt. If you can ask the question in a matter-of-fact tone of voice, and without appearing judgmental, you can encourage others to focus on their own behavior.

Another example:

Parent: Johnny never comes when I call him.
Psychologist: When you ask Johnny to come and he doesn't, what do you do?

How did (do) you feel about that?"

The feelings of the individual are often a significant clue to what happened in a situation, particularly in a situation involving conflict. Feelings are often a response to the behavior of others. By asking about feelings you can often get a better understanding of the other person. An example:

Boss: We may have to upgrade our computer facilities.
Employee: How do you feel about that?
Boss: Well I'm concerned about the cost, but it could really help us out and maybe save money in the long run.

Another example:

Speaker: I'm not sure whether to buy that house or not. There are just so many factors involved.
Listener: How do you feel about it?
Speaker: Well, I really like the house, I'm just not sure I want to go into debt any more.

What is it that ... ?

There are situations where image-centered criticism, whether it be self-criticism, criticism of third parties, or direct criticism made of you, interferes with problem solving. By turning a vague criticism into a question, you can often elicit a more problem-centered response. We will first look at how to ask for specifics when confronted with vague criticism (Lange and Jakubowski, 1978; Smith, 1975).

Critic: You are so irresponsible.
Response: What is it I haven't done that is causing a problem? [Incorporating vague criticism into a question asking for specifics.]

Notice that the response does not assume you agree with the other person's assessment, but only that you want to get his or her point of view. Some people feel that asking a question like this implies that they are in agreement with the speaker, but instead, it invites a more specific reply by assuming the other person's perspective.

Let's look at another situation. In this situation, a boss attempts to intimidate an employee:

Boss: Can't you do anything right? Good grief!
Response: What is it I haven't done right? [Incorporating vauge criticism into a question asking for specifics.]

At this point, the boss will either come up with a substantive issue or back off. Again, keep in mind that even though the response asks the question from the critic's point of view, the response does not necessarily imply agreement with that point of view. The employee has only accepted that such-and-such *is* the critic's point of view, and not that it is true.

The goal of asking for specifics when you are under fire is to stay focused on the problem—or at least to find out what the problem is. When you are working with others your goal is not simply to cope, but to cope in a way that leads toward problem solving. In the following example, an irate student is upset about a test:

Irate: Your last test was really unfair.
Response: What is it that makes the test unfair? [Incorporating vague criticism into a question asking for specifics.]

The response is not simply a way of coping with a hostile student, but is a way of getting additional information. The teacher does not necessarily accept the student's judgment, but he does want to find out what the student thinks about the situation. This might lead to the student's changing his behavior, to the teacher's making some changes in his methods, both, or neither. Regardless of the outcome, the more information the teacher has, the more appropriate his response will be.

The essence of this approach is to ask for specifics that relate to solving problems instead of defending yourself. Treat all criticism, regardless of how image-centered it sounds, as if it were problem-centered (Martin, 1979a).

There are times when you may want to solicit problem-centered criticism from others without opening yourself up to attack. Asking for specifics allows you to get information about your own performance without becoming upset. The advantage of such information is that you understand the other person's position, even if you don't agree with it, and you are in a position to negotiate with the other person about the issues that are raised. In the following dialogue, a listener is confronted with a problem concerning her own actions:

Client: I don't feel like you're really helping me much. I don't feel any different when I leave here.
Listener: You're not satisfied... [Reflecting]. What is it I need to do to help you? [Asking for specifics.]

Chances are that the client doesn't really know what he wants, but he may have enough of an idea that at least the listener has a starting point for discussing the problem.

When you ask for specifics of a criticism, you are still free to judge your own behavior and what (if anything) you want to do about it.

Encouraging others to be specific about their criticism of others

You can also use the "What is it that...?" formula when image-centered criticism of a third party interferes with focusing on a problem.

Teenager: My parents are impossible. They're always getting on me. If they would just leave me alone, things would be a lot better.
Listener: What is it they do that makes them impossible? [Turning a vague criticism into a question asking for specifics.]

This question encourages the teenager to analyze what he doesn't like about his parents' behavior by asking the questions from the teenager's point of view without taking sides.

Encouraging Others to Be Specific About Self-criticism

When self-blame and criticism keeps others from focusing on a problem, you can use the "What is it that...?" formula to encourage problem-centered specifics:

Self-critic: I'm stupid. I can't do anything right! [Image-centered self-criticism.]

Listener: What is it you did that isn't right? [Inviting a problem-centered statement by asking for specifics.]

By asking for specifics in this way, you avoid contradicting the other person's feelings (thus avoiding a power struggle) while getting specific information about the problem.

FOLLOW-UP QUESTIONS

Follow-up questions are particularly useful when you have asked for specifics (or the other person has volunteered them) but the answer is still vague.

Can you give an example?

This question is useful when the other person describes a general situation without providing details. For example:

Parent: One problem we have with Mike is his irresponsibility. I wish I knew what do about it.
Counselor: Could you give an example of his acting irresponsible?
Parent: Yes, ... he is supposed to take out the garbage, but I usually end up doing it.

The counselor now has a specific situation that parent and counselor can discuss. Through further questioning the counselor can learn what actually happens in this situation and what the parent might do differently.

Can you be more specific?

This is another excellent follow-up question to use when you get a vague answer. An example:

Client: My wife doesn't cooperate when I want to do something.
Therapist: Can you be more specific?
Client: Like when I want to get out of the house on a Saturday night, say.

The last reply is still vague, but the client is beginning to be more specific.

In what way?

This question is often useful and can be used interchangeably with the previous two questions. An example:

Friend: My boss is really unfair!
Listener: In what way?
Friend: She has asked me to come in two Saturdays in a row and I have already done more than a lot of other people.

In three words, the listener encourages the friend to talk about a specific situation that bothers him, without creating defensiveness in him. This is much better than asking a question likely to produce a defensive response (for example, "Why do you say that?")

CHOOSING A COURSE OF ACTION

Once the relevant details of a problem have been established, a course of action needs to be chosen. In Chapter Eleven we will look at how to use the skill of asking for specifics to get others to take responsibility and make decisions (Strategy 3). In using this strategy you can pick and choose from the questions that follow, as the need arises. Choosing a course of action involves helping others make value judgments, examine consequences, state what they want, and, the final step, make plans and decisions. We will look at questions that are useful in taking the other person through each of these steps.

Making Value Judgments

Solving problems often requires value judgments about the present situation and about what is wanted. If you want others to make decisions and take action, first get them to make a value judgment about the present situation and about what they are doing to make that situation better or worse. Questions that focus on the individual's responsibility for making value judgments include:

- Are you making things better or worse?
- How is what you are doing helping the situation?

- Is what you are doing helping you?
- Is what you are doing helping others?

These questions need to be asked in a way that doesn't imply judgment, but that encourages the other person to think through the problem.

Are you making things better or worse?

This is a question I learned by watching Rudolf Dreikurs, a well known Adlerian psychiatrist. Every bad situation can be made worse. People who complain about their situation may have a legitimate complaint, but unless they focus on their own responsibility for making the situation better or worse, they have no possibility of changing that situation. Example:

Client: I know I complain a lot to my wife about the way she keeps the house, but I feel like I've got a legitimate gripe. She really doesn't keep things cleaned and picked up and it really burns me up when I get home at night.

Helper: Well ... does what you say to her make the situation better or worse?

Client: Well, I suppose it doesn't help, but I feel like she has it coming.

Helper: Assuming you are right that she does have it coming, how does your behavior help the situation?

Client: Well I suppose it doesn't. I know it doesn't; it's just that I get so frustrated with the situation.

The client is now at a point where the helper can encourage him to consider changing his own behavior. Until the other person realizes that his behavior is not helping the situation, you are not going to be effective in encouraging him to change.

Focusing on Consequences

A sense of power and responsibility both develop from the experience that decisions and actions have consequences. You do something and you see a result; if you don't see any result, eventually you no longer feel responsible for what happens; you no longer feel you can affect what happens; you are powerless.

Helping others see that their actions do have consequences (good or bad), gives them a basis for making decisions, and also the sense of power necessary for assuming responsibility. The following questions are useful in encouraging others to focus on consequences:

- What are the likely consequences?
- How do you think that will work?
- What's likely to happen?
- What's the worst possible thing that could happen?

In the following example a listener helps a woman think through a problem. By helping her examine the consequences of different alternatives, the listener helps her build a basis for a decision:

Woman: I've thought a lot about going back to work even though Carrie is two years old. I'm not sure what to do.

Listener: You want to go back and yet have mixed feelings. [Reflecting previous discussion and present feelings.]

Woman: That's right. I know what the alternatives are, I just am having trouble deciding.

Listener: What are the likely consequences if you do go back? [Asking for specifics, focusing on consequences.]

Woman: Well, Carrie would go to a nursery school, which would be good for her, though it would be better if she didn't have to stay all day. I wouldn't have as much time around the house to do things that need to get done—cooking, things like that.

Listener: How about your relationship with Charlie (her husband)? [Asking for specifics; focusing on consequences.]

Woman: Well he says it's up to me, but I can tell he feels uneasy. He would adjust pretty well, though. I don't think there would be any long-term problems.

Listener: Charlie would adjust... [Reflecting]. What would be the consequences with Carrie? [Asking for specifics; focusing on consequences.]

Woman: That would be a real problem. I don't want to give up the time I spend with her, but I do want time away from her and I think the nursery school would be good for her a couple of hours a day.

Regardless of what she decides, she is thinking about the consequences of different alternatives and is clarifying her feelings about them.

Exploring Worst Possible Consequences

Helping others make decisions by having them explore the consequences they fear most is a useful approach developed by Albert Ellis (1971, 1977). When people avoid making decisions because they fear dire consequences, this avoidance may be based on realistic expectations, or (more often) it may be based on an irrational fear of consequences that are extremely unlikely. You can sometimes help others deal with irrational fears by helping them explore the consequences they fear most. Rational consideration of the probable risk is sometimes necessary to get individuals to take even the smallest action. When people put their fears into words and then examine them, they often find their fears are irrational. They are then free to choose to act in spite of their fears. When people feel uneasy about things they haven't examined, this uneasiness keeps them from acting in situations where no real danger exists or where the dangers involved are acceptable. The following dialogue illustrates the technique:

Reluctant: I've always wanted to learn to ski.
Listener: I am wondering what keeps you from learning.
Reluctant: What, at my age? I would feel really foolish.
Listener: Well, how old are you?
Reluctant: Twenty-five.

Perhaps this conversation sounds silly, but I have heard similar reasoning from nineteen-year-olds—and fifty-year-olds. What *Reluctant* fears in this situation is not the physical danger, but failing or looking stupid. Here is a continuation of the dialogue using the techniques of reflecting and focusing on consequences:

Reluctant: I've always wanted to ski... I don't know why I don't. I feel like I'm too old to start now. [An irrational statement that needs to be examined.]
Listener: You sound disappointed...
Reluctant: Yeah...
Listener: What's the worst possible thing that could happen? [Focusing on consequences.]
Reluctant: I don't know. I could kill myself, I suppose, but that doesn't seem likely. I could break my leg—more likely, but the thought doesn't really scare me.
Listener: But you'd like to... [reflecting]. There seems to be something else bothering you about doing it.

Reluctant: I'd feel foolish being out there with a lot of people who can ski and I'm just starting.
Listener: People meaning young women?
Reluctant: Uh huh. I think that's it.

Nothing has yet been solved in this conversation, but *Reluctant* is now in a much better position to decide what he really wants to do. Other situations where this approach may be useful include:

- Doing something you want to do but are not sure you can succeed at.
- Beginning or ending a relationship.
- Changing jobs.
- Changing lifestyle.
- Asking for a raise.

Encouraging Others to State What They Want

Asking others what they want can be a useful way of getting others to focus on their own wants and needs. We will look at two questions that do this:

- What do you want?
- What do you want to see (*hear, feel*)?

What do you want?

"What do you want?" is a favorite of busy people. It gets immediately to the point. Effective administrators, businesspeople, therapists, teachers, and others use this question to save time, especially when the other person has trouble coming to the point.

People strongly oriented to the wants of others may know what they could do to meet the expectations of others, but feel powerless because they don't consider their own wants. Such people need to ask themselves, "What do I want?" This is particularly important for people who think they have to do things because they're expected to. People who consistently ignore their own desires in order to meet expectations eventually come to resist making decisions and to drag their feet implementing decisions that have been made.

There is a variety of reasons why people don't take their own desires seriously, including:

- Past experiences suggest that the best way to protect oneself from disappointment is to avoid personal involvement in decisions.
- Desire to please others.
- A mistaken sense of responsibility toward others, toward an idea, or toward a set of rules or policies.

What do you want to see (hear, feel)?

These questions are useful in getting others to imagine what they want. Some examples: "I never hear anyone praising my efforts." "What would you want to hear?"

Another example: "I just can't see myself doing that job." "What can you see yourself doing?"

A third example: "I don't know how to feel about her wanting to move to Florida." "How would you like to feel?" Notice that in each case the listener's reply uses the same verb as the speaker. This is important. If a speaker is using verbs that refer to *visualizing,* using a verb that refers to hearing or feeling is going to disrupt the speaker's thinking process (Bandler and Grinder, 1975, 1976).

Encouraging Others to Make Plans and Decisions

At some point coping with a problem calls for making choices about specific steps to be taken. People often muck around in their problems without ever deciding what they are going to do until the decision is made by default. Appropriate questions can encourage others to examine alternatives and make choices:

- What can (could) you do about it? [Focusing on making a plan.]
- What are you going to do about it? [Focusing on responsibility; emphasis on making a decision.]

What can (could) you do about it?

This question is useful in encouraging the other person to explore alternatives without trying to make a decision right away:

Client: I want a better job. I am sick of the one I have now.
Helper: Yes, you've said that several times today. What could you do about getting a different job?

Even though this question may be threatening at first, it encourages the client by assuming that she can do something, that she is not powerless.

What are you going to do about it?

This question puts the responsibility on the other person to make a decision. It also allows you to sidestep responsibility for problems that don't belong to you. This question is particularly effective when others imply that you *should* accept responsibility for their problems.

Student: I don't have a pencil! [Implying the teacher should do something.]
Teacher: What are you going to do about it? [Asking for specifics; focusing on student's responsibility for taking care of the problem.]

Instead of giving the student a long lecture about being responsible (and then giving in by giving the student a pencil anyway), the teacher allows the responsibility to remain with the student.

"What are you going to do about it?" is also a good way to get a commitment from someone who has good intentions about changing, but who avoids action.

Person A: I would really like to lose some weight. I just can't seem to stick to a diet. I just need to eat less, I guess.
Person B: Well, what are you going to do about it?

A word of warning: if the other person has not asked or does not want help, such a question may easily provoke a negative reaction.

SUMMARY

By asking questions that focus on the specifics of a problem and what can be done about it, you encourage others to focus on items that can be discussed rationally and productively. Questions that focus on *what* the problem is are much more likely to result in problem-centered discussion than questions that focus on *why* there is a problem.

The essence of encouraging others to accept responsibility is to focus on the present situation and on what the individual can do about it. Questions that focus on specifics tend to encourage others by communicating the assumption that they can make decisions and then act on them. Such questions, however, need to be used with caution and in a noncoercive way.

chapter six

Skill four: Making I-statements: Getting across your own concerns, needs, limits, and feelings

Our culture encourages us to beat around the bush when asking for what we want, setting limits, saying what we think, or telling others how we feel. Avoiding direct statements seems safer, more polite, and easier, but in the long run deprives both you and the person you are talking to of the mutual power that develops from being clear, direct, and concrete. When talking about your own feelings, wants, needs, decisions, or responsibilities, a simple sentence beginning with "I" has the advantage of being:

- Direct where other sentences are indirect.
- Concrete where other sentences are theoretical.
- Clear where other sentences are ambiguous.

For example:

Indirect: *Everyone* is concerned about you!
Direct: *I* am concerned about you.

"Everyone is concerned about you" is indirect, theoretical, and evasive. (Who is "everyone"?) In contrast, "I am concerned" is direct and unambiguous; both speaker and listener know exactly what is meant.

If you want others to trust you, to say what they think and feel, and to accept responsibility for their problems, then you need to speak openly and directly when talking about your own thoughts, feelings, and problems. I-statements allow you to do this (Alberti & Emmons, 1978; Jakubowski & Lange, 1978; Lange & Jakubowski, 1976).

I-statements are often the most direct and effective way to:

- Express appreciation.
- Say what you think without arguing or putting others down.
- Set limits by saying what you're willing to do.
- Express anger and frustration.
- Confront others when you have a problem (three-part I-message).
- Accept responsibility for mistakes.
- Ask for what you want.
- Express care, concern, and love.

While the three skills we have considered in previous chapters focus on encouraging others to speak clearly and directly, this chapter focuses on expressing your own ideas, feelings, and concerns using I-statements.

Basic Principle

When talking about your own feelings, wants, needs, or responsibilities, use "I."

There are things we need to say or want to say that cannot be said without using "I"—or we end up saying something else. For example, "You are loved by me" is not the same as "I love you," even though one is a grammatical transformation of the other. We experience statements such as "You are loved" as mere statements, but we experience I-statements such as "I love you" as decisions and actions in themselves.

EXPRESSING APPRECIATION

The other day while sitting in a restaurant I overheard a conversation between a salesman and the manager of a store a few doors down. In the midst of talking about orders for cassette tapes, gift items, and such, the manager threw in something about himself:

Manager: I was really sick last night—headache, throwing up, the whole thing. . . . I feel like I shouldn't even be here.
Salesman: I appreciate your getting up . . .
Manager: Oh well . . . (and they went back to business)

In these few words, the two of them established a point of contact. All it took was a few seconds.

I-statements allow you to express your appreciation of others in a simple, direct way. Expressing appreciation lets others know that you value them. Examples:

- Thanks for the ride. I appreciate your going out of your way.
- I admire your courage.
- I enjoy working with you.
- I'm glad I married you.

At times we take for granted that people we live and work with understand that we do value and appreciate them without our having to express that appreciation. Not expressing your feelings denies the other person information needed to know how to respond to you. When one person denies another knowledge of his own feelings he may prevent the relationship from growing. For example, a husband who does not express his feelings discourages his wife from sharing her feelings. We learn to accept and value ourselves through being accepted and valued by others. Expressing appreciation teaches others that they are valued and appreciated.

Appreciation is based on acceptance rather than on evaluation Appreciation is very different from a positive evaluation. When you praise others, you are evaluating them or their performance, and such evaluation may be threatening (Dinkmeyer and Dreikurs, 1963). When you express appreciation, you are sharing your feelings with another person. The most common complaint that people have is that they are not appreciated. If you want to develop a relationship with someone, let him know how you feel. People can value one another in a relationship without any regard to accomplishment or success. A parent and child can value and appreciate one another without regard for any accomplishment on either side. The same may be true for friends.

Expressing appreciation encourages increased openness in communication
The more openly you express appreciation of others, the more likely they are to feel secure about sharing their feelings. We are most guarded in what we say when we feel unsure about how we will be received. People will sit for hours talking about nothing, and then in the last few minutes of a visit somehow find a way to say what they really think and how they feel about one another.

Expressing appreciation may make sense in close personal relationships, but what about relationships on the job? An almost universal feeling that people have about the work they do is that "People don't appreciate my efforts." We live in a society where people find it very difficult to encourage one another. Expressing appreciation is a way of encouraging others by not taking for granted those things that we do value in them.

SAYING WHAT YOU THINK WITHOUT ARGUING OR PUTTING OTHERS DOWN

I-statements can allow you to state your own position, values, or preferences without getting into a power struggle or putting others down. You don't need to argue with others in order to state a different viewpoint, conclusion, or preference. Using I-statements allows you to state your own viewpoint in a direct, straightforward way without arguing or attacking the other person. The problem with arguing or attacking other viewpoints is that the emotion becomes the focus of attention; others stop listening to the content of what you are saying and pay attention only to the emotional tone of the conflict. Stating your point of view in a way that encourages others to listen is more productive than trying to convince others that you are right. Example:

You Statement: How can you say that closing this school is going to help education in this district?
I-Statement: I think closing this school is going to hurt the education of the children in this neighborhood.

The listener in this example lets the speaker know his position without arguing or attacking the speaker.

SETTING LIMITS BY SAYING WHAT YOU ARE WILLING TO DO

Setting limits is often difficult. It is particularly difficult to set limits in situations where we want other people to like us, to cooperate, to see us in a positive light. It sometimes seems easier to avoid setting limits, leading people (often unintentionally) to believe that they are going to get more from us than we are willing to give.

If you lead people to believe that they may get more from you, you invite their harassment for as long as they think they have a chance of being successful. When they find out they're not going to get what they had hoped for, they leave feeling resentment for what they didn't get, instead of gratitude for what they did get. People's feelings about you depend not only on what you do, but on what they have been led to expect. Not setting limits invites misunderstanding and resentment on both sides.

I-statements allow you to state what you're willing to do. When you state calmly and politely what you are willing to do, others will tend to accept it and to go on from there without resenting you or thinking any less of you—even when they disagree with the position you take. Examples:

A: Can you reschedule my appointment on Thursday?
B: I can't see you at another time on Thursday; next Monday would be possible. [I-statement: setting limits.]
A: Yes, but I've got things planned for that day and I'm leaving town on Tuesday.
B: I would be willing to see you on Thursday, as we scheduled, or after you come back from your trip. [I-statement: setting limits.]

By stating what she is willing to do, *B* is able to set limits without arguing.

The secret to setting limits is to focus on what she will do, not on trying to make the other person change. By saying what you will do, you put the other person in the position of having to respond to your statement. When you try to change the other person, you make it easy for the other person to defeat you by objecting or refusing to cooperate.

Don't depend on the goodwill of others not to take advantage of you. It is your job to set reasonable limits. No one can take advantage of you unless you allow it, and no one can be blamed for attempting to get whatever they can from you if you, by your ambiguity, encourage them to believe they might get more than you are willing to give.

EXPRESSING ANGER AND FRUSTRATION

I-statements allow you to state anger and frustration without acting out those feelings (e.g., by blaming or threatening others) (Cotler and Guerra, 1976; Jakubowski & Lange, 1978). Feeling anger and frustration creates a bind: If you keep those feelings bottled up, you feel upset and are apt to act less effectively as a result; if you let out the feelings in an uncontrolled way, you are likely to say or do something you regret later. In any case, feelings cannot be successfully hidden; they come out in tone of voice, facial expression, and other nonverbal behavior. Useful ways of expressing anger and frustration without accusing the other person include:

- I don't like that.
- I resent your doing that, please stop.
- I resent having to wait half an hour for you.
- I don't like being put down.

Such expressions allow you to accept responsibility for your anger and frustration without blaming others. Tone of voice is important; if your tone of voice implies blame the other person will perceive your statement as a blaming statement, regardless of the words you use. The following example illustrates using I-statements to express anger and frustration in a way that encourages problem solving.

Employee: I am really upset about your changing my assignment and I need to talk to you about some problems that have resulted as soon as possible. [I-statement: expressing frustration.]
Supervisor: It couldn't be helped and I really didn't think you would mind.
Employee: I feel really upset about your changing my assignment and I especially resent not being asked or at least consulted. [I-statement: expressing frustration and resentment.]
Supervisor: I didn't realize this was going to be a problem. Maybe we'd better sit down and talk this over....

Employee is now in a position to negotiate using the other skills presented in the book. But what if the boss says, instead, "Do it or resign!" or threatens to fire you?

- You are still in a better position than you would otherwise be. You now have a better idea of where you stand, which puts you in a better position to decide what you want to do about your situation.
- Even if the supervisor doesn't like what you say, as long as you are not hostile in the way you express yourself, you are not an immediate threat and are very unlikely to get fired. As long as you don't create a power struggle and give the other person no reason to exercise power against you, the other person has no reason to use his power.

Some readers may be thinking, "Yes, but isn't saying you are angry a power play?" The answer is no—as long as you stick to I-statements and don't approach him in a hostile manner, or make demands or threats that give him an excuse to refuse the demands or counter the threats. Sure the supervisor is going to feel uncomfortable, but his feeling uncomfortable is not a sufficient reason for him to fire you—and his feeling uncomfortable may encourage him to negotiate.

Formal relationships follow rules; as long as you follow the rules, the other person has a strong tendency to also follow those rules. As long as you follow the unwritten rules that structure your relationship, the other person almost has to respond in a predictable way. Of course, there are no guarantees and you must be willing to consider the likely consequences of your actions and then act accordingly. I-statements, like all the other techniques in this book, are alternatives, not commandments.

CONFRONTIVE I-STATEMENTS (GORDON'S THREE-PART I-MESSAGE)

When you have a problem because someone else's behavior is unacceptable, a confrontive I-statement focusing on *your* problem can be an effective way to enlist the other person's cooperation without putting him or her on the defensive. One type of confrontive I-statement is what Thomas Gordon calls an I-message. The essence of an I-message (Gordon, 1974) is that you own the problem by stating the specific effect the other person's behavior is having on you and how you feel about it. When other people understand that you have a problem, they are much more likely to cooperate than they are when you attack them.

When other people's behavior causes you a problem, the tendency is to blame or attack them, putting them on the defensive and insuring that you won't get their cooperation. Accepting responsibility for the problem ("I have a problem. . . ." instead of "you are creating a problem. . . .") is more likely to get results, especially if the statement includes:

- A statement of the specific behavior that is causing the problem: "When you do X. . . ."
- A statement of how the speaker feels about the situation: "I feel Y (upset, frustrated, angry, concerned, etc.). . . ."
- A statement of the specific, concrete effect the problem behavior is having on the speaker: "Because the effect is Z."

An example:

When you don't get your work in on time . . . [statement of specific behavior] I feel frustrated [statement of specific feeling] because I have to spend extra time [statement of specific, concrete effect on speaker].

It doesn't make any difference in what order the elements occur, but it is important that all three elements be present. It is also useful, at least at first, to construct I-messages using the formula already given:

When you do X, I feel Y because the effect on me is Z.

This formula may seem artificial and contrived, but it has been my experience that it is essential in learning the technique. Without a formula, it is too easy to construct statements that seem to be I-messages, but that are really manipulative and guilt-inducing statements. Let's examine each of the three parts of an I-message in more detail.

Statement of the Specific Problem Behavior

The more specific you make the statement of the problem, the less likely it is that the other person will be defensive. As Chapter 2 demonstrates, the more general a criticism, the more it sounds like an attack and the more threatened the other person will tend to feel. Adjectives such as *irresponsible, lazy, stupid,* and so on, are especially likely to generate defensive reactions. The following examples show the difference between problem-centered and image-centered statement of the problem behavior. The problem-centered examples are almost always going to be more effective.

Problem-centered: When you leave the car windows open at night ...
Image-centered: When you can't even close the car windows ... [Accusing.]

A second example:

Problem-centered: When you are late for your appointment ...
Image-centered: You are always late for your appointments ... [An accusation; eliminate *always.*]

A third example:

Problem-centered: When you don't have your work in on time ...
Image-centered: When you *never* get your work in ... [Too general; an accusation; eliminate *never.*]

Statement of Your Feelings

Use "I" to say how you feel. By stating your feelings you are in effect accepting responsibility for the problem. It is important to say "I feel *y*" rather than "you make me feel *Y.*"

Direct: I feel frustrated ...
I feel upset ...
I feel uneasy ...
Indirect: It upsets me ... [avoids responsibility for the feeling; easily sounds like an accusation.]
You make me angry ... [blames the other person for your feelings.]
It is really frustrating ... [Focuses on "it" rather than on "I."]

The purpose here is to communicate your feelings, not to lay blame.

Statement of Specific Effects

State the specific unacceptable effects on you. (Note that your feelings do not count as a concrete effect because you are responsible for your feelings.)

Specific   ... Your smoke gets in my eyes.
Effect: ... I have to mop out the car when it rains.
              ... I have to spend extra time.

Not   ... I feel I am not doing a good job. [Not a specific effect, but
Specific: your feelings.]
              ... You might get in trouble. [Not an effect on you.]

No matter how concerned you are about what others are doing, if their behavior is not actually having a concrete effect on you, an I-message is not effective. For example, "When you smoke, I feel really concerned because I am afraid of your getting cancer" is not likely to be effective because your being concerned or upset is not a concrete effect caused by the other person; you choose to feel concerned. On the other hand, if smoke is blowing in your face and you say, "Your smoke is blowing in my face, and I feel uneasy because I am allergic to smoke and am likely to react to it," it will probably lead to a problem-centered response.

Here are additional examples of complete three-part I-messages:

- When you don't set the table on time, I feel upset because I can't serve dinner when it's ready. (Good example of concrete effect.)
- When you don't talk about your problems until the last ten minutes of our session, I feel frustrated because I can't do much to help you in ten minutes. (Effect is not as concrete as previous example, but worth a try.)

ASKING FOR WHAT YOU WANT

I-statements are particularly useful when you need to ask for something (Jakubowski & Lange, 1978, 157-158). This skill is a difficult one to practice, but is one of the most valuable.

You will find the following phrases useful in being direct about asking for what you want:

- I want ...
- I need ...
- I would like ...

If you begin a sentence with any of these phrases, the phrase almost forces you to be direct. Reasons for being direct include the following: The busier the other person is, the more he or she will appreciate your being brief and direct. You are more likely to get what you want if you ask directly. Even if you don't get what you want, the other person will respect you for your directness and appreciate your not wasting his or her time. I continue to be amazed at how easy it is to get help from other people if you know what you want and know how to ask for it. Most people feel flattered to be asked for help—if they are being asked to provide something they can give.

The following examples demonstrate direct and indirect ways of asking for something.

Situation: You are asked to take on additional responsibilities that you are willing to do, but you would like to be paid for the additional work and responsibility.

Indirect: Of course I'll do it. I hope you'll consider this when I come up for promotion.
Direct: I would like to do it; I would also like to be paid for the additional work and responsibility and would want to work out an agreement before I start the new assignment.

In the indirect statement, the speaker expresses an interest in getting a raise without actually asking for it, thus giving the boss a chance to avoid the issue without actually saying no. In the direct statement, the boss either has to say no right out or negotiate. Even if the boss says no, you are in a better position because the boss knows you expect to get paid for what you do and you know where you stand. Particularly in situations where people ask you to provide services without expecting to pay, you have to decide what you are willing to do or not do. You may provide whatever services you wish free of charge, but you also have a right to ask that your needs be met—including your monetary needs.

Another example:

Situation: You need to change an appointment with a client.

Indirect: Do you really need to see me next week? I was planning on going out of town and it would be really helpful if you would come another day.
Direct: I would like to change your apointment to another day next week. I will be out of town on the day of our appointment.

The indirect statement may get the job done, but it is unnecessarily indirect and it puts the responsibility on the other person for saying that he or she doesn't really need to see you. In the direct statement, you accept the responsibility for asking for what you want. The other person doesn't really have a choice in this situation, so it is manipulative to pretend that he does.

EXPRESSING CARE, CONCERN, AND LOVE

I-statements can be a direct and effective way to communicate caring, concern, and love (Alberti & Emmons, 1978). While such expressions are normally reserved for close personal relationships, they are very similar to expressing appreciation and are often appropriate in a wide variety of situations. Caring and concern for others often develops in both helping and working relationships. Unfortunately it is easy to avoid expressing concern, and other people don't know how you feel if you don't tell them. Men in particular are programmed to avoid showing or talking about their feelings, especially feelings of caring, concern, and love. Changing this pattern can be hard work. Unwillingness to express caring is sometimes based on fear: fear of looking weak, fear of rejection, fear of being vulnerable. The greater the degree of programming, the greater courage it takes to express one's concerns. It takes courage to make an I-statement and say, "I care. I'm concerned."

Examples of I-statements:

- I care.
- I'm concerned.
- I trust you.
- I love you.
- I care what happens to you.

Sometimes we don't express our feelings because we feel it's risky. The more you are willing to take risks, the more secure you will feel in taking those risks. The more open you are, the less you will fear being open.

WHEN TO AVOID "I"

Prefacing ideas, observations, and opinions with phrases such as "I believe," "I think," "I feel," "In my opinion," and so on, does not make them into

I-statements, and these phrases may undercut what you have to say and soon become repetitious:

Unnecessary I think I would like to work with you.
Use of "I":
Better: I would like to work with you.

Adding "I think," "I feel," and so on to sentences that are already I-statements may undercut them. Another example:

Unnecessary I think I am willing to help you.
Use of "I":
Better: I am willing to help you.

Another inappropriate use of "I" is to tell the story of your life (unless asked to do so). Particularly if others are there to solve their problems, they may not want to listen to your experiences. Stories that begin with "Let me tell you what happened to me when I was in that situation..." are not always welcome.

Using "I" when giving instructions or directions is also inappropriate. "Would you please do X?" is usually preferable to "I want you to..." Such phrases sound authoritarian and provoke resistance.

SUMMARY

I-statements allow you to state your own needs, feelings, limits, problems, and concerns in a direct way without creating conflict. Clear I-statements encourage cooperation.

The most important element we bring to a relationship is ourselves and our willingness to treat others as people instead of objects. I-statements, even confrontive I-statements, are a way of giving something of yourself. People will tend to trust you when you are open with them. They will tend not to trust you in a situation in which they are vulnerable and you are not. Your I-statements encourage others to take the risk to also be open.

chapter seven

Skill five: Focusing on an area of agreement

When others attempt to put you on the defensive, the skill of focusing on an an area of agreement is useful in getting the other person to focus on the problem rather than on you.

All of the skills can be used to avoid responding defensively; Chapter Thirteen on dealing with conflict will demonstrate how to do this. The skill of focusing on agreement is particularly useful when someone makes a blaming, accusative, or guilt-inducing statement. Agreeing with the other person without giving in deflates the other person's attack while leaving the door open to a more problem-centered discussion. We will look at three ways of accomplishing this:

- Agreeing in part—agreeing with that part of a statement that you can agree with.
- Giving information without contradicting—answering an attack by stating what is true without contradicting the other person or making yourself a target.
- Admitting mistakes—meeting an attack that is substantially true by admitting your mistakes without acting defensive.

Basic Principle

*If you refuse to fight,
others cannot fight with you.*

Fighting is a way for some people to cope with a situation in which they don't feel they have any alternatives. When you recognize that you are becoming involved in a power struggle, you can use *focusing on an area of agreement* to avoid both fighting and giving in.

AVOIDING A POWER STRUGGLE BY AGREEING IN PART

Agreeing in part allows you to avoid arguing or acting defensive by agreeing with that part (and only with that part) of a statement that is true:

Irate Parent: You've been working with my daughter for three months and I don't see that she is any different.
Professional: We haven't seen the changes we would like to see. [Focusing on an area of agreement by agreeing in part]

Agreeing with that part of a statement that is true allows you to avoid arguing. Willingness to disagree, to confront, and to cope with confrontation are important in many situations. Agreeing in part is not a substitute for confronting or responding to confrontation. However, when the purpose of a question or statement is to provoke you into a power struggle, no rational discussion is going to come out of disagreeing.

In responding to a message, respond first to emotions, then to the problem. When messages have a strong emotional content and a problem content, you will be more effective by first responding to the emotional content. Until the other person has calmed down, rational discussion will be difficult, and the other person is unlikely to listen to you.

In the following situation, an irate individual comes to an employment counselor upset about not having a job after two months of searching.

Counselor: ... You are finding it difficult to find a job.
Client: You aren't much help. I've been coming here regularly for a month and you have yet to come up with anything.

Counselor: You have come in and there haven't been any openings that fit you. [Focusing on an area of agreement by agreeing in part.]

By agreeing with the client without accepting blame for the situation, the counselor can defuse the situation.

Agreeing without accepting blame accomplishes two things: (1) It avoids reinforcing the client's behavior. (2) It helps the counselor reestablish a sense of perspective, a realization that "Mr. Smith is understandably upset about not having a job—I don't have to accept responsibility for his being upset. This is not really a personal attack: I don't need to feel or act defensive." By learning to act less defensively, the counselor feels less defensive.

What happens if the counselor, irritated by the client's words and tone of voice feels, "What right does he have to blame me, I've done what I can." As soon as she feels this way, she has been sucked into a pattern of negative cooperation by the client. The incident may be trivial but if it happens several times a day, and each time the counselor finds herself feeling upset, these small incidents will soon result in her feeling frustrated and burned out.

Don't agree with value judgments. You can agree with the facts of a situation without agreeing with value judgments. This is especially important when you find yourself in the position of being judged by others.

Remaining the judge of your own behavior allows you to avoid the impossible task of trying to fulfill contradictory expectations. If you relinquish your right to judge your own behavior, you allow yourself to be made powerless. As long as you do not accept the other person's right to judge you as a person, you retain your power to make decisions and to act on them. An example:

Irate: You are obviously incompetent if you make that kind of a mistake. How could you?
Listener: I could have handled the situation better. [Agreeing with the facts without agreeing with the value judgment.]

The listener responds in a sincere, but nondefensive tone of voice. Even though he does not argue with the other person's judgment, he refuses to agree with it or accept it.

Another example:

Supervisor: Are you still using all this human relations stuff with the people you work with? I don't believe in all this listening and compromising. You've got to exert your authority.
Employee: As I learn to use the skills, I find I am able to work with people effectively. [Stating facts without accepting value judgment.]
Supervisor: Well, I wouldn't use it.
Employee: It's an approach not everyone feels comfortable with [focusing on an area of agreement by agreeing without accepting value judgments.]

To avoid a fight while maintaining the other person's respect, you need to communicate your respect for the other person's point of view without apologizing for your own. A power struggle may result if a superior feels his or her position and status are threatened by your way of doing things. In such a situation, an excellent strategy is to communicate that you are not questioning your superior's position and status, but that you will continue to act in ways you find to be effective.

Giving in may be interpreted as subservience and does not increase your boss's respect for you. Fighting may work but will often place you at a disadvantage because the boss usually has more power, and a power struggle gives him or her an excuse to use it. Particularly when supervisors must rely on your judgment, they will often go along even though they don't agree—if you handle the situation well. Agreeing in part without accepting an unfair value judgment is one way to avoid both fighting and giving in.

GIVING INFORMATION WITHOUT CONTRADICTING

Giving information without contradicting the other person allows you to cope with a person who insists on fighting with you or who attempts to put you on the defensive by asking questions of the "Do you still beat your wife?" variety.

Example:

Parent: You people let the kids get away with murder. Why has there been more trouble this year than any year I can think of?
Educator: There has been a lot of trouble this year. [Focusing on an area of agreement by stating facts without contradicting.]

By not responding to the attack, a power struggle can be avoided.

In using this skill, however, be careful not to use sarcasm or the technique may backfire, as in the following example:

Parent: You people let the kids get away with murder.
Educator: Yes, I can see how you might feel that the kids get away with murder. [Agreeing, but using a sarcastic tone of voice.]
Parent: (Becomes even more angry and starts to make threats.)

In the following example, an irate father wanted to argue about whether his daughter, now living with his ex-wife, needed counseling and whether the therapist could provide any help. This was a no-win situation in which the father had made up his mind about the situation and was there to impress his view on the therapist.

Father: You can't do anything for Susan unless you change her mother first. [Challenging, argumentative tone of voice.]
Therapist: I am working with Susan and her mother to help Susan cope with school. [Focusing on an area of agreement by stating facts without contradicting.]
Father: Well, if her mother wants help, she'll have to pay for it herself.
Therapist: Of course. I see Susan's mother only in connection with helping Susan. [Focusing on an area of agreement by stating facts without contradicting.]

In this situation, the therapist did not change the father's ideas. Nevertheless, by sticking to the facts, he avoided being pulled into an argument that would accomplish nothing.

Giving information without contradicting is also a useful technique to use when the other person has a legitimate concern but is using an image-centered rather than a problem-centered approach. If you ignore the tone of voice and answer questions nondefensively, you can sometimes encourage a more problem-centered approach:

Teacher: We are using a learning center approach for some subjects this year.
Parent: Well, it looks like play to me. What are the kids learning anyway? [A legitimate question, but stated as an accusation.]

Teacher: The students do enjoy the centers. [Agreeing in part without accepting value judgment.] The centers are designed to meet a variety of objectives in writing, science, and math. If you would like to look through the projects your son has been working on, I can show you what he is learning. [Giving information without contradicting.]

The parent's question is somewhat hostile, but the interest in knowing what the child is learning is quite legitimate. By ignoring the hostile tone and responding nondefensively to the parent's concerns, the teacher keeps the situation problem-centered.

ADMITTING MISTAKES

When you are accused of making a mistake you have in fact made, the quickest and easiest way to short-circuit an image-centered attack is to admit the mistake. It is important, however, to do this without inviting or accepting blame and without acting defensive. This is best done by admitting the mistake without making excuses and without giving lengthy explanations.

Examples:

You're right, I am late for our appointment. Shall we get started? [Admitting mistake; focusing on the task at hand.]

Another example:

When I said I would help you, I may have given the wrong impression. I am willing to look over your work, but not to do it for you. [Accepting responsibility for possible mistake.]

A third example:

Yes, I did reschedule you to work on Saturday after I had promised you the day off. That was my mistake. What would be a fair way to solve this? [Admitting mistake and offering to compromise.]

MISGUIDED ATTEMPTS TO AVOID POWER STRUGGLES

Certain approaches may avoid conflict at the cost of long-term effectiveness.

Avoiding Dialogue

Repeated use of focusing on an area of agreement can be used to avoid answering others' questions. For example, members of certain sects (for example those you may meet on streetcorners or in airports) will avoid an argument by refusing to answer your questions or statements if you disagree with them. A more subtle form of this behavior can be found where a person appears to listen very carefully, but ignores what you have said. An example of this is a supervisor who listens with great interest and encourages you to believe that your views will be taken into account and then habitually acts with complete disregard for what was discussed. Using the techniques to avoid answering legitimate questions can be an effective way to avoid responsibility, but it also short-circuits cooperation and may easily provoke a power struggle.

Using a Sarcastic or Condescending Tone of Voice

Agreeing in a sarcastic or condescending tone of voice will tend to encourage a power struggle rather than prevent one. Sarcasm can be effective in squelching an attack, but it generates defensiveness and resentment in the other person.

SUMMARY

A continuing pattern of power struggles requires cooperation. You can successfully cope with such a pattern by not reacting defensively. Focusing on an area of agreement allows you to do this. The essence of focusing on an area of agreement is to stay problem-centered. By not reacting to personal attacks, accusations, or manipulation, you encourage the other person to focus on the problem rather than on you.

part three

STRATEGIES FOR USING THE SKILLS IN COMBINATION

You can best prepare for a situation by having in mind a strategy for organizing the skills. The next six chapters demonstrate how to combine the skills from Part II into five strategies:

- Listening
- Helping others think through problems
- Getting others to accept responsibility and make decisions
- Negotiating when you have a problem
- Staying problem-centered when attacked

These strategies are ways of organizing the skills in particular situations.

chapter eight

The five strategies

A strategy is a plan of action. Choosing and rehearsing a strategy allows you to prepare a plan of action and then to respond flexibly and without locking yourself into predetermined (and often inappropriate) responses. The strategies are ways of planning how to use the skills to achieve specific goals.

STRATEGY 1: LISTENING

Strategy 1, *listening*, uses *reflecting* (Skill 1) and *responding nonverbally* (Skill 2) to achieve four goals:

- *Establish rapport.* When you show others that you are willing to listen, you invite them to say what's on their mind.
- *Involve others by encouraging them to talk.* The key to motivating others is to get them to participate.
- *Collect information.* Listening is an excellent way to get the information you need to understand a situation and to make decisions about it.
- *Gain time to make a decision.* Listening gives you time to think about what to do next.

Listening means not merely hearing the words, but allowing yourself to view the world from the other person's perspective, without judging or evaluating. It's easy to make the mistake of jumping to conclusions, and then giving your own opinions before you understand what the other person is trying to say. Listening and then reflecting offers an excellent strategy for understanding.

STRATEGY 2:
HELPING OTHERS
THINK THROUGH PROBLEMS

Strategy 2 is actively assisting another person in thinking through a problem by reflecting the specifics of the problem, value judgments, and alternatives necessary to help the other person reach a decision. Strategy 2 is a low-key, nonthreatening way of assisting people who want to talk about problems.

STRATEGY 3:
GETTING OTHERS
TO ACCEPT RESPONSIBILITY
AND MAKE DECISIONS

Strategy 3 is using the skill of asking for specifics to encourage others to accept responsibility for problems and make decisions about what they can do. This strategy assumes that you want to take an active role in helping others confront problems, accept responsibility, generate alternatives, and make decisions. It is an excellent strategy to use when you are willing to use a more confrontive approach to problem solving than Strategy 2. Strategy 3 is an excellent strategy to use when both you and the other person want to save time in solving a problem.

STRATEGY 4:
CONFRONTING OTHERS
WHEN YOU HAVE A PROBLEM

Regardless of the helping or problem-solving roles you assume, there are times when you need to set limits to the help you are willing to give, when you need to confront others' unacceptable behavior, or when you need to negotiate an agreement. This strategy differs from the other four in that it requires you to focus on your own attitudes, limits, feelings, and needs. It is particularly difficult because it calls for confronting others by using I-statements about how you feel, about what you are willing to do, about what you find to be a problem. We easily incline toward using the word "you" when we want to confront others with a problem we are having.

STRATEGY 5:
STAYING PROBLEM CENTERED
WHEN ATTACKED

You need to know not only how to handle attacks and resistance, but how to encourage others to rationally discuss their legitimate concerns. It is relatively easy to counter attacks; it is much more difficult to listen to the legitimate concerns that often underlie them and to turn the conversation to the consideration of those concerns.

This is a strategy that is almost always used in conjunction with at least one other strategy. Once you succeed in redirecting the discussion to the problem, you can then move on to the most appropriate of the other four strategies.

PROBLEM OWNERSHIP—
DECIDING WHO HAS THE PROBLEM

Effective use of the strategies depends on your ability to determine who has the problem—you or the other person. The principle of problem ownership (Gordon, 1974) is a tool for deciding when something is your problem and when it is the other person's problem. This is important because how you choose to deal with a situation depends on who has the problem.

Basic Principle:

A situation is your problem when it has a direct and unacceptable effect on you.

A situation that does not have a direct and unacceptable effect on you is not your problem, though you may have a responsibility to take action.

It is my belief that long-term working, helping, and problem-solving relationships are not possible unless you observe the distinction between what is your problem and what is the other person's problem. I emphasize this point deliberately because many people believe that they can help or work with others only by taking on their problems.

The two examples that follow clarify the concept of problem ownership. The first example concerns smoking, the second, suicide. I use the example of smoking because it is an example familiar to everyone. I chose the second example, dealing with a threat of suicide, because it shows the use of problem-ownership at work in an extreme case.

Example No. 1:
Concern About
Someone Who Smokes

Consider the following situation—you know someone who smokes. It's not good for her health; she knows it and you know it. You are concerned; you care about her, but under the principle of problem ownership her smoking is clearly not your problem. Confronting her and trying to force her to change is not going to work very well, no matter what skills you use. Her smoking has no direct, unacceptable effect on you unless she is blowing smoke in your face. When she does blow smoke in your face, then her behavior does have a direct and unacceptable effect on you and you definitely have a problem—not a serious problem, but a problem nonetheless. In this situation, you can use the skills to confront her in a friendly way and you can probably reach a solution agreeable to both.

Example No. 2:
A Threat of Suicide

Unlike the example of smoking, working with someone who wants to commit suicide is outside the experience of most people. The principle of problem ownership, as practiced by professionals who work with suicide cases, may throw light on other, less consequential situations.

Accepting responsibility for solving the problems of someone who threatens suicide is putting oneself in an untenable position. The person who does this accepts responsibility for something over which he has little or no control: someone else's life. In addition, by accepting responsibility for another's life, he puts himself in the power of another person—saying in effect "I will allow my life to be controlled by your threats and actions." This is a disastrous position for both helper and client. No matter how much a helper may be willing to help, only the client can accept responsibility for his or her own life. Although we will examine the problem of responsibility in problem ownership in greater detail in Part Four, at this point we need to consider the practical consequences of the principle of problem ownership in choosing a strategy.

CHOOSING A STRATEGY

Knowing how to choose which of the five strategies is appropriate at a particular moment is important. For example, listening may be very effective by itself when others want to talk about their problems, but it is often not sufficient in situations where the other person wants and needs help in solving a problem.

Choosing a strategy requires answering three questions relating to problem ownership:

* Who has the problem?
* What does the person with the problem want?
* What are you willing to do?

The following guidelines show how the answers to these three questions can be used to choose a strategy.

Use Strategy 1 (Listening) When:

* The other person has the problem or you're not sure who has the problem.
* The other person wants you to listen or you are not sure what the other person wants.
* You are willing to listen.

Comment: Listening is a good choice in the opening stages of just about any conversation.

Use Strategy 2
(Nondirective Problem-solving) When:

- The other person has the problem.
- The other person wants someone to act as a sounding board in thinking through the problem.
- You are willing to help the other person think through the problem.

Comment: This is a good choice when you don't have any direct responsibility for the other person.

Use Strategy 3
(Getting Others to Accept Responsibility and Make Decisions) When:

- The other person has the problem.
- The other person wants help or at least agrees to interact with you.
- You are willing to help or have a responsibility to confront the other person in regard to the problem.

Comment: This strategy is especially useful when you have responsibility for working with the other person.

Use Strategy 4
(Negotiating with Others) When:

- You have a problem.
- You want the other person to make a change that will help solve your problem.
- You are willing to ask for what you want, are prepared to set limits, or both.

Comments: This is the strategy of choice when you need to ask for something or when you need to set limits.

Use Strategy 5
(Staying Problem-centered
When Attacked) When:

- You have the problem of someone attacking you or attempting to engage you in a power struggle.
- You want to turn the attack into a problem-centered discussion.
- You are willing to discuss the problem but not to engage in a fight or give in.

Comment: This strategy allows you to remain calm under fire while attempting to proceed to one of the other four strategies.

INCREASING SPONTANEITY

People sometimes fear that becoming aware of their behavior and consciously choosing how they are going to act will take the spontaneity out of their lives. The opposite is the case. When you are aware of what you are doing, you have a choice—you are free to do something else. You are not condemned to repeating the same actions over and over. Similarly, when you recognize self-defeating patterns in others, you can use the strategies to help them become aware of and then change their behavior.

SUMMARY

These five strategies bridge the gap between knowing the skills and using them in problem-solving situations. The strategies allow you to plan how you want to handle a situation without locking yourself into predetermined (and possibly ineffective) actions. The strategies also provide alternatives in situations where no preparation is possible and thinking on your feet is necessary. The next five chapters present the strategies in detail.

chapter nine

Strategy 1: Listening

Strategy 1 is encouraging the other person to talk by listening and using the skills of reflecting and of responding nonverbally with attentive silence and listening cues. It is the most simple of the strategies, and is probably the most useful, yet is often the most difficult to practice.

When to Use

- The other person has the problem.
- The other person wants you to listen or you are not sure what the other person wants.
- You are willing to listen.

Goals

- Establish rapport.
- Get the other person involved (motivated).
- Get information you need to proceed.
- Give yourself time to make a decision.

The Strategy

Use skills 1 (reflecting) and 2 (responding nonverbally) to:

- Reflect the other person's main message.
- Respond nonverbally with attentive silence and listening cues.

Simply listening to another person is sometimes the most difficult of the five strategies, perhaps because it often means listening without trying to solve something. In situations where there is no solution or where you can't help solve a problem, you help most by listening. I think that one of the most persistent misunderstandings about working with other people is that helping others means bringing about a solution. In some cases this is true, and most of the examples in this book do involve changes. However there are many ways to help others that do not lead to solutions. Listening can give others:

- The opportunity to express and share feelings.
- The knowledge that someone cares enough to listen without judging.
- The knowledge that someone understands a problem, even though he can't do anything about it.
- The encouragement to cope better with a situation that cannot be changed.
- The feeling of being treated as a human being rather than as an object.

When I demonstrate the listening strategy in a group, someone from the group may ask, "Yes, but you haven't solved her problem. How have you helped?" We all need people with whom we can share our fears, joys, doubts, and anguish. Yet it is easier to turn away rather than listen to another person talk about a problem about which we can do nothing. In such situations, willingness to listen creates a bond with others.

EXAMPLE 1: LISTENING TO PEOPLE WHO ARE HIGHLY MOTIVATED TO TALK*

A person who is highly motivated to speak may need little verbal feedback. The transcript that follows is a fragment of a longer conversation. The listener

*Excerpted from a student transcript; used with permission.

writes about the dialogue,

> "It seemed that Donna was extremely eager to pour it all out and get it out of her system. There were very few pauses. Any kind of interruptions or questions would have been roadblocks."

In the conversation, Donna talks about being away from home:

Donna: ... Okay, I decided to go to college after high school. I applied to two colleges.

Deb: Uh huh.... [Inviting discussion by responding nonverbally—listening cues.]

Donna: My mom was trying to treat me really nice and she helped me go to the stores and pick out stuff that I needed—an extra toothbrush, etc....

Deb: Uh huh. [Responding nonverbally—listening noises.]

Donna: And everything else. She was really helpful, except in the last week before school started, everything I did was wrong. She'd ask me to clean the house, it wasn't clean. And I had to cook dinner all the time. I didn't make the right thing. Everything I did was wrong, so I thought my mom was just upset because I was leaving. The first day I was at college I was so embarrassed. I'll never forget when I walked up to the dorm. First of all we drive up here and I brought my boyfriend. He's twenty and he's in the family, sort of. He wants to leave home, but has no idea how to do it yet. So he's, like, in my spot. I think I am as mature as he is....

Deb: Uh huh. [Responding nonverbally—listening noises.]

Donna: .... when I walked into the dorm, I had no idea of where everything was at. I saw this big long line waiting to get rooms and stuff like that. And Mom goes (raises her voice) "Donna, you make sure you have this" and "Donna, make sure you have that." And I go, "Yeah, Mom, I know, I know." You know how you answer moms back (sarcastically).

Deb: Uh huh. [Responding nonverbally—listening noises.]

Donna: My mom walked to the car and pouted, and then my Dad went after her. Then my Mom and Dad started to walk towards the stadium and my Mom's telling Dad that I don't love her anymore, that their eighteen-year-old daughter has no care for her and everything like that. She thought I was ... (pause)

Deb: Drifting away or something. [Reflecting—summarizes underlying message.]

Strategy One: Listening / 105

Donna: ... because she thought I was trying to go away I didn't pick the college closest to home. I should have gone to the junior college in my town 'cause that was the closest. I should have gone there but I had to leave home.
Deb: I see. [Responding nonverbally—listening noises.]
Donna: Then she got this really stupid idea that I didn't love her any more. I couldn't see myself in her place; so maybe I didn't understand.

Comment: Donna is beginning to consider the situation from her Mom's point of view; not that she agrees with it, but she takes it into account in understanding the situation. Reflective listening is often useful in helping a client reach this kind of insight, but in this case it was unnecessary.

Deb: Uh huh. [Responding nonverbally—listening noises.]
Donna: I got a letter in the mail two weeks later that made me cry. My Mom had written a letter (raises her voice again, "Donna, I think you're going through the parent syndrome, where you don't care for me anymore." etc., etc.,
Deb: Uh huh. [Responding nonverbally—listening noises.]
Donna: ... A lot of these things add to my mother's problems. When she was a little girl first her mother died. And then her father went to war and died too. She got passed around the relatives and got stuck with a family that didn't want her. They didn't want her around, so they'd lock her up in the closet—for hours and hours. So, that's where my Mom got the inferiority complex that she's ... (pauses to think).
Deb: That she's not acceptable. [Reflecting, drawing implications.]
Donna: Yeah, Mom has a hard time getting accepted with people ... (continues to talk about her mother).
Deb: Uh huh. [Responding nonverbally, listening noises.]
Donna: I still go home, do what she wants me to do, give her an extra hug when I reach home. But I don't wanna think about it and still try to be nice to her. She's getting used to Donna not being around. I do my studying and try not to think about it ....

Donna sees her mother's viewpoint, but also her own. In this dialogue, the client, Donna, has talked about her problems and realizes that she is already coping with them as well as she can.

EXAMPLE 2: LISTENING TO PERSONAL CONCERNS*

The following dialogue is between a parent and teenage daughter. The parent listens to the daughter talk about her interest in a boy she has met at a camp. This is precisely the sort of situation where many parents fail to establish rapport because they ask probing questions. While the conversation is about a small, even trivial matter, by listening and reflecting the parent finds that the daughter is much more open about talking and sharing with her in other situations as well.

Parent: Did you say you had something you would like to talk about? [Inviting discussion.]

Daughter: Yes.

Parent: What did you want to talk to me about? [Second invitation to discussion.]

Daughter: Well—there is this guy—I didn't really meet him at camp. I'd met him before I went to camp. And when I was at camp, I kinda, oh . . . I decided I kinda like him, but I don't know how to get his attention.

Parent: You don't know how to get his attention. [Reflecting; repeating key sentence.]

Daughter: No, he is a pretty shy guy and this other girl told me that he's not a guy that likes—well, he likes the girls, but he's just not a guy that goes out a lot. But—he's kinda quiet and . . . I don't know.

A relationship may stand or fall on the ability to listen and respond in a nonjudgmental way.

COPING WITH PROBLEMS VS. SOLVING PROBLEMS

Not all problems have a solution; not all situations can be resolved. Problems concerning relationships, money, the meaning of one's life, illness, and death, often have no solution other than learning to deal with them. What gives people a sense of power over their lives is not that they can control things, but that they can continue to think and feel and act and not be paralyzed

*Excerpted from a student transcript; used with permission.

by the problems that face them. When others come to us with problems and situations that cannot be resolved, we can sometimes encourage them by listening.

Being Available Without Forcing

Make yourself available, but don't try to force others to make use of that offer. Sometimes the most difficult task in a relationship is waiting until the other person is ready to talk. By letting the other person know you are available without attempting to coerce the other person, you leave the door open.

GUIDELINES

In using Strategy 1, the following guidelines are useful:

- Avoid asking questions except to clarify your understanding. Even the skill of asking for specifics is often better not used at the beginning of a discussion.
- Say as little as possible. If the other person wants to talk out a problem, the less you say, the better. Use the skills of responding nonverbally with attentive silence and listening cues.
- Focus on the message, not on the words. Pay attention to the overall communication—spoken and unspoken. Use reflecting when needed to communicate that you understand.
- Avoid trying to help solve the problem, at least until you think the other person wants or is willing to accept help.

SUMMARY

Listening to others and encouraging them to talk by using reflecting and responding nonverbally is an excellent strategy to use when another person comes to you and wants you to listen. It is a strategy that good listeners use naturally without thinking about it. It is also a useful strategy for avoiding the trap of trying to solve problems that cannot be solved. In the next chapter we will look at how to use the skills of reflecting and responding nonverbally to help others think through those problems that can be solved.

chapter ten

Strategy 2: Helping others think through problems by reflecting: Non-directive problem solving

Strategy 2 is useful in encouraging others to think through problems. You do this by listening and reflecting the specifics of a problem and what can be done about it. Strategy 2 uses the same skills as Strategy 1, but with a different goal in mind: encouraging the other person to solve a problem.

When to Use

- The other person has the problem.
- The other person wants you to act as a sounding board in thinking through the problem.
- You are willing to help.

Goal

- Help the other person think through a problem where you want to supply a minimum of direction.

The Strategy

Use Skill I (reflecting) to:

- Reflect the specifics of the problem.
- Reflect value judgments.
- Reflect alternatives.
- Reflect decisions.

You will find that unless the other person is willing to accept your help, the strategy of reflecting the specifics of the problem and what the other person can do about it may (often correctly) be interpreted as interference. Strategy 2 is an extension of the first strategy, but whereas Strategy 1 can be used in almost any situation in which someone wants to talk, Strategy 2 requires that the other person be willing to work on the problem.

A person solving a problem will usually be concerned with the specifics of the problem, his or her own feelings and value judgments about the problem, possible alternatives, and choosing a specific alternative. By knowing in advance that at some point each of these four areas are likely to arise, you can be ready to use your reflecting skills to facilitate the process. Using reflecting in this way is a low-key way of keeping the other person on task and is particularly useful with people who want help but are likely to feel defensive. By being nondirective you encourage the other person to think through a problem in a nonthreatening way. Using Strategy 2 also helps you, because by being nondirective you avoid taking on responsibility for problems that don't belong to you.

Strategy 2 is also an excellent one to use when a problem is not well-defined and the goal is to explore the problem rather than to solve it. The advantage of this strategy is that it lets you be flexible. This strategy will help you to avoid missing key points in the other person's efforts to think through a problem.

The examples that follow are divided into segments according to four steps of the strategy: (1) talking about the specifics of a problem, (2) making value judgments, (3) considering alternatives, and (4) making decisions. The four steps exist to help you orient yourself in encouraging the other person to think through a problem. These steps need not be in order and a conversation need not include all four steps.

EXAMPLE 1:
ENCOURAGING RESPONSIBILITY*

Being able to encourage other people to accept responsibility for what they do about their problems is one of the most useful skills you can have. When people concentrate on what is happening *to* them rather than what they are doing, they tend to see themselves as being acted upon rather than acting. Encouraging others to change this perception requires encouraging them to focus on what they can do, rather than on what is being done to them. By reflecting others' concerns about their situation, and particularly their uncertainty about what they can do, you can encourage them to think about what they can do rather than what is happening to them. By clarifying and summarizing others' problems, you can help others see the situation accurately, see what can be done, and decide what to do about it.

The following example is a transcript of a conversation between an adult, Marsha, and a child, Tommy.

Adult: Something seems to be bothering you... [reflecting feelings; the other person doesn't need to speak for you to reflect nonverbal messages.]

Child: Oh, it's just that Mrs. Boone isn't very fair... (pause) she got mad and took away my recesses for the rest of the year.

Reflecting Specifics of the Problem

Adult: You feel this isn't fair. [Reflecting feelings; drawing implications.]

Child: No. And neither does my mother. She came to school the other day to talk to the teacher and she talked the teacher into letting me have recess as long as I turn in my homework from now on.

Adult: She took your recesses away because you didn't hand in homework. [Reflecting; drawing implications.]

Comment: Notice that the adult does not take sides. What the teacher did may make little sense to the adult, but taking sides will not help the child solve his problem.

*Excerpted from a student transcript; used with permission.

Child: Yes, but I just haven't had time to do it all and besides I don't always hear her give assignments on account of I'm out of the room when she gave the assignment.

Adult: And you feel Mrs. Boone is being unfair by not telling you when you get back to the room.... [Reflecting child's view of the situation—summarizing.]

Child: Yeah, I mean it's not my fault if I don't know about the assignments, is it? [Looking for agreement.]

Adult: (Waits silently for child to continue.) [Responding nonverbally —listening cues.]

Comment: Silence allows the helper to leave responsibility for the situation with the child. Taking sides with the child or with teacher would not help the child assume responsibility for the problem. Whether the teacher is right or wrong, the child will have to deal with the situation as it is, not as the adult in this dialogue would like it to be.

Child: ... Mrs. Boone says I should ask if there is anything assigned but I forget to, sometimes... (pause) besides I don't like homework to ... well, I don't get to play.

Comment: Here is the crux of the situation. The child would like to avoid responsibility for his homework. The adult refused to go along with this, but she doesn't lecture.

Adult: You get tired of being inside and studying and not playing. [Reflecting implications; summarizing.]

Child: Mother says I have to do my homework so I don't have to stay in at recess to do it like Carol, but that's different (pause, then laughs).

Adult: Um huh... [Listening noises, nonverbal encouragement.]

Child: Mother is pretty upset and she says she is going to have a talk with Mrs. Boone but I don't really want her to 'cause it'll just make Mrs. Boone mad or something. What should I do?

Reflecting Alternatives

Adult: You are not sure what to do. [Reflects question back to child.]

Comment: This statement has much the same effect as a responsibility-centered question such as, "What are you going to do about it?"

Child:	No. I wish I did though. (pause)
Adult:	(Waits silently). [Nonverbal encouragement: silence.]
Child:	I guess it couldn't hurt anything if I was to talk to her myself, right (pause)? I think I will try that, and if it doesn't work maybe my mother needs to talk to her (pause). All I really care about is going out for recess. I hate not getting to play outside. Yeah, I will talk to Mrs. Boone myself. Do you think that's a good idea?
Adult:	You think that talking to Mrs. Boone would be the best thing for you to do. [Reflecting subject matter, avoids reassurance, which is asked for, but which would take responsibility away from Tommy.]
Child:	Yeah (nodding head). My time is just about over isn't it? I think I'll talk to her while the kids are out 'cause I have to stay in anyway. (Bell rings, time for Tommy to leave.) Bye, and wish me luck. (Laughs, lightly.)

Reflecting Decisions

Adult: I'm glad you reached a decision. [I-statement.]

This dialogue is not the usual way in which adults work with children, nor is it the usual way for the adult in this transcript. She writes about herself:

> Most of the time in the past I have given my advice as to the way I thought Tommy should handle a certain problem. I realize now that I was not doing very much to help him learn to help himself. In this conversation I feel I was able to be more of a help to him than all the other times in the past. . . . By paraphrasing I was able to let him rehear what he was saying to me and think things through for himself. The use of paraphrasing helped me understand what he was saying to me and made it easier and unnecessary for me to give him the advice I had in the past, advice he really didn't need, thus giving him a chance to make up his own mind and solve his own problems.

Tommy starts out complaining and placing the responsibility on the teacher. When Marsha does not take sides, and instead reflects Tommy's concerns, he begins to think about the problem and what he can do. Using reflective listening, he begins to focus on the problem.

EXAMPLE 2:
HELPING OTHERS THINK THROUGH PROBLEM OWNERSHIP*

A common situation in working with people is that others will come to you and want to solve a problem but are confused about what is their problem and what is not their problem.

In the following situation, a listener is approached by a friend wanting to sort out responsibility for a problem.

Friend: I'm having a real mess with this friend of mine who is going to school. She and her husband are working on their masters'. He has left her and is seeing another woman. She is really upset and I feel really responsible because I encouraged them to go back to school. She is an old friend and she relies on me for her support. This is upsetting to me because I'm not always there where she needs me. [Mistaken ownership of problem.]

Reflecting Specifics of the Problem

Listener: Mmhmmm. So you feel very involved right now because you encouraged her to go back to school. [Reflecting.]

Friend: Right. I feel it is partly my fault. I also feel bad because I don't think I would put up with what she does from her husband. I really can't say this to her. [Mistaken problem ownership.]

Listener: You really care about her and have a lot of concern right now about what she is going through. [Reflecting feelings.]

Friend: She has gone through a lot. Her father died. Her husband almost left her a year ago. She doesn't have many friends right now.

Listener: You are really taking a lot of the responsibility on your own shoulders. [Reflecting implications.]

Friend: (Gives a little laugh.)

Listener: (Laughs.)

Friend: She comes around all the time, which is getting on my husband's nerves. I wish I could help more.

*Excerpted from a student transcript; used with permission.

Reflecting Value Judgments

Listener: You've been trying, by what you've been saying, but it really involves you more than you want at the present time. [Reflecting implications; clarifies friend's ambivalence about the situation.]

Friend: Right. We only have a certain amount of time to deal with things like that....

The problem is not yet solved, but several things have been accomplished: First, the listener has avoided taking on her friend's problem as her own. Second, the listener has acted as a sounding board for her friend, and her friend has a better understanding of the situation. A more confrontive style might be helpful in encouraging the friend to examine her own role in complicating her life, but the listener has not been hired to provide this kind of help.

EXAMPLE 3:
HELPING OTHERS THINK
THROUGH PERSONAL PROBLEMS

Using reflecting to help others think through personal problems often involves helping the other person become more aware of the *process* of how he thinks about the problem. In the following example, the emphasis is on what is going on inside the person with the problem rather than on the problem itself. At the point where this dialogue picks up, helper and client have already spent a considerable amount of time discussing the situation.

Client: ... So that's how it is, and there is nothing I can do about it.

Reflecting Specifics of the Problem

Helper: You are convinced there is nothing you can do. [Reflective listening; paraphrasing.]

Comment: The choice of what to reflect focuses on the client rather than on the situation at this point. By stating what is obvious in a simple and direct way, the helper draws the client's attention to what he is doing.

Client:	Not really. What do you think? Do you think I can do anything?
Helper:	That's what we're here to find out.... [Problem-centered statement.]
Client:	I feel like it's useless to even try.
Helper:	So... my impression is you are resigning yourself to the situation, saying, just accept it, it's hopeless, I can't do anything. [Reflecting: drawing out implications of client's previous statement.]
Client:	Well, that's why I came here—to get some help.

Reflecting Value Judgments

Helper:	You do want to make things better. [Reflecting: drawing out implications.]
Client:	Yes, otherwise why am I coming here?
Helper:	You do want help. [Reflecting.]
Client:	Yes, I just don't see what I can do.
Helper:	It would be very disappointing to get your hopes up and then nothing happens. [Reflecting; drawing implications—a hypothesis about what client is feeling.]
Client:	Well, sure... (silence).
Helper:	You don't want your hopes dashed. [Reflecting; summarizing.]
Client:	I don't want my hopes dashed. They've been dashed too many times already. I don't want to have to go through that again.
Helper:	... so you make sure you won't have to go through it again... [Reflecting—drawing implications.]
Client:	How? I don't see that.

Comment: The helper is beginning to draw together the threads of the client's two contradictory attitudes: he wants help and he doesn't want to take any chances.

Helper:	I'm not sure. You can avoid having your hopes dashed by not attempting to do anything [Reflecting]. Is it possible that this is what is happening?
Client:	Well... I suppose so... yes. It's just that I have been through so much already....
Helper:	I can understand that. [I-statement—giving support.]
Client:	What can I do?

Helper: You see, now, at least a little bit, how you are defeating yourself.... [Reflecting; summarizing the situation.]
Client: Yes, I think so.

Reflecting Alternatives

Helper: ...But you're not sure what you can do.... [Focusing on responsibility for making plans.]
Client: Stop thinking there's nothing I can do.
Helper: O.K. I think you've got a place to start now....

The client has begun to see something of his own attitudes and how he is defeating himself.

EXAMPLE 4:
ASSUMING AN ACTIVE ROLE*

The following example is based on a demonstration I did in front of a group. Fred, a member of the group, wanted a demonstration of using reflective techniques in a more active way. I asked him to talk about something that was bothering him and he talked about a situation that had occurred several weeks before and that was still bothering him. Fred's neighbors had been giving a party, the party got noisy, someone called the police, and Fred was blamed. As the dialogue opens, Fred is explaining that he was falsely accused.

Fred: ...and my neighbor said, "Well, the only reason we called the police is because you called 'em on us a couple of months ago when we had a party. The police came to our door and I know that you're the one that called because you were the only one that was in the apartment building at the time." And I said, "Well, I'm sorry but I have never called the police on anybody and I wouldn't." I said, "If I think you're making too much noise I would feel like I could come down and tell you or call you." And he said, "Well, I'm sorry but we were just trying to get back at you. That's the only reason we called the police. We won't do it again. Good-bye." And I was just, ah, I didn't know what. And I know he thinks I'm lying. I wish I could find out

*Excerpted from a transcript made by the author with a graduate student; used with permission.

who really did it, because I could just tell, or I think I could tell, from the tone of his voice that he didn't believe me. And I hate it when people think I'm not telling the truth or when people think that I would do something like that.

Reflecting Specifics of the Problem

Bob: So the thing that's really bothering you is the fact that he doesn't believe you. [Reflecting implications.]

Fred: Right. And he thinks I'd do something like that in the first place.

Bob: That's bothering you—that you're a terrible person because you would call. "Somebody must think I'm a terrible person that I would do this thing." [Reflecting implications.]

Fred: Yeah. I don't like people to be upset with me, and I especially don't like people to think I'm lying—especially when I know I'm not. But I don't know how to prove it.

Bob: So . . .

Fred: What should I do?

Reflecting Alternatives

Bob: So that's what you're kind of saying, "Well gee, what should I do to prove that I am a good neighbor, and here I went to all the trouble to be a good neighbor and now I don't know what to do." [Reflecting implications—summarizing.]

Fred: Right. But I know that it shouldn't bother me. I mean I, I know that it shouldn't bother me because I know myself that I haven't done anything wrong as far as, you know, calling anybody on them and I realize that I should, or I think I should, just go on and think of it as if it's their problem. I know it's their problem.

Bob: Intellectually . . . [Reflecting content.]

Fred: Right, but emotionally it's hard, you know.

Bob: You're saying: I can't stand it when people get upset. [Reflecting implications.]

Fred: Right. Right.

Bob: So there's just, it's a . . .

Fred: Conflict.

Bob: Conflict within you. [Reflecting feelings—repeating.]

Fred: Uh huh. But I'm sure in a few weeks it will pass.

Bob: If you just wait.... [Reflecting content—paraphrasing.]
Fred: Yeah.
Bob: It will all blow over.... [Reflecting content—paraphrasing.]

Reflecting Specifics of the Problem

Fred: But it's hard to deal with right now.
Bob: So you try to sort it out. [Reflecting implications.]
Fred: Uh huh.
Bob: The intellectual on the one hand, "This really shouldn't bother me." On the other hand, it really does. [Reflecting content—summarizing conversation thus far.]
Fred: Yeah.
Bob: It's hard to deal with. [Reflecting content—summarizing conversation.] Is there anything else you want to say about it? [Invitation to continue.]
Fred: No. I let it all out. It makes me feel better to talk about it. I asked a friend if he could find out who had turned them in to the police so I could go to them and say, you know, just kind of pushing it in their face, "See, I didn't do it," you know, and I know that would do no good because it would probably just cause more problems.
Bob: You'd like to get even with them for getting even with you for something you didn't do. [Reflecting implications.]
Fred: Right. Or if I could just prove that they're wrong. But that would only worsen the problem, I'm sure. So I know it's just best to be left alone, but I almost dread to see them, you know, like in the, coming in and out of the apartment. I just don't like to even run into them. I don't that often, but, like, I kind of am avoiding it now.
Bob: So you're upsetting yourself even when you don't see them. [Reflecting feelings.]
Fred: Yeah.
Bob: So that's really the problem. It's not so much the problem with the neighbors—that's over—but rather in you. [Reflecting implications—summarizing conversation.]
Fred: Right.
Bob: It's still bothering you even though you almost never see them. [Reflecting feeling—summarizing.]
Fred: Right.

The important point to make about this dialogue is the creative role that reflective statements can make in clarifying a problem. When the conversation begins, Fred does not really understand what is going on between himself and his neighbors. As the conversation goes on, he begins to see that much of the problem lies within himself, that he is making assumptions about how his neighbors *should* act—assumptions that only end in feelings of resentment and frustration because he can't control what his neighbors think or do. The feedback statements that are made are not mere paraphrases and summarizations of what Fred has been saying; they restate Fred's concerns. Bob's statements show Fred not merely what he has said, but his thinking process. Once Fred sees his thinking process, he is in a position to say: "Oh, now I see what I'm doing to myself. That doesn't make sense: I don't have to do that to myself."

SUMMARY

Listening and reflecting allow you to give feedback in a way that helps establish rapport while encouraging others to examine both their problems and their way of thinking about those problems. By reflecting the specifics of the problem, the other person's value judgments about the problem, the alternatives, and, finally, a decision, you can keep the other person focused on problem solving. Strategy 2 is particularly effective in situations in which a low-key, relaxed approach is wanted. In the next chapter we will look at a more direct (and also more confrontive) way to encourage problem solving.

chapter eleven

Strategy 3: Getting others to accept responsibility and make decisions: Directive problem solving

Strategy 3 is a direct, and at times confrontive, way to get people to accept responsibility, make decisions, and take action. Based on the *reality therapy* model developed by William Glasser (Bassin, Brattler, & Rachin, 1976; Glasser 1965, 1969; Gazda 1975), Strategy 3 is particularly useful in situations in which you are in a position of responsibility. Strategy 3 is an effective, noncoercive way to get others to accept responsibility by getting them to determine the specifics of the problem, make value judgments, make decisions, and carry out those decision.

When to Use

- The other person has the problem.
- The other person wants help or at least agrees to interact with you.
- You have a responsibility to confront the other person.

Goal

- Encourage others to accept responsibility and make decisions.

The Strategy

Use skill 3 (asking for specifics) to:

- Identify specifics of the problem.
- Get a value judgment.
- Generate alternatives.
- Ask for a decision.

The goal of Strategy 3 is to find a way to get another person to confront a problem and to accept responsibility without your getting in the way. In this respect, Strategy 3 is no different from Strategy 2, where your goal is to encourage others to think through problems, accept responsibility, discover alternatives, make decisions, and follow through on them. Where Strategy 2 uses a more nondirective approach based on the skill of *reflecting*, Strategy 3 relies primarily on the skill of *asking for specifics*.

In particular, attempts to change others in ways they don't want to change leads to power struggles; once in a power struggle the other person has sufficient reason to avoid facing his problems: by refusing to face them, he defeats you. The essence of using Strategy 3 to confront others is saying what needs to be said as simply, gently, and directly as possible. Particularly when there is a need to confront someone with a problem situation, the desire to avoid unpleasantness sometimes leads to hinting and beating around the bush in the hope that difficulties can be handled without unpleasantness. Unfortunately, taking what seems to be the easy way out often results in trouble later on. Being effective requires simple, direct, honest communication. Although it often requires facing unpleasant problems, situations, and emotions, it does not require *acting* unpleasantly. If the other person doesn't want help, using this strategy can create a power struggle. However, if you have even minimal cooperation, Strategy 3 can be a powerful tool for change.

EXAMPLE 1:
HELPING OTHERS
CONFRONT BEHAVIOR
THEY WANT TO CHANGE

In the following example we will consider how to use Strategy 3 to encourage a person who wants to give up smoking to actually quit. I chose this example because it is a touchy problem that concerns millions of people. Let's use the following example to illustrate how you might go about using Strategy 3.

122 / STRATEGIES FOR USING THE SKILLS IN COMBINATION

Imagine you know someone named John whose heavy smoking concerns you. Assume that John seldom smokes in your presence, so John's smoking has no direct affect on you.

Before you even choose to use Strategy 3, you need to consider who has the problem. Determining who has the problem is important because different strategies are required if the problem belongs to you rather than to the other person. When you have the problem (e.g., smoke in your face), your objective is to meet your own needs. When the other person has the problem (e.g., John wants to quit smoking) your objective is to assist him in solving his problem.

A good way to bring up the subject might be to state your own concerns about John's smoking. Stating your concerns is more likely to be effective than judging or blaming and putting others on the defensive. Any attempt to coerce John by making him feel bad or act defensively will only create resistance.

If John doesn't want help, you can't manipulate him into wanting to discuss the matter, and attempting to do so will only lead to resentment. Once you have let John know about your concern, what he does then is his responsibility, and if you respect him, you don't take what is his responsibility on yourself.) A dialogue with John, using Strategy 3, might go something like this:

Identifying Specifics of the Problem

You: John, I'm concerned about your smoking. [I-statement.]
John: (somewhat defensively) I know it's not good for me. I just can't stop. I've tried and it doesn't work.

Getting a Value Judgment

You: You would like to give up smoking, but you haven't been able to do it. [Reflecting—summarizing situation.]
John: It's almost impossible. Very few people ever succeed. [Making excuses, inviting helper to rescue.]
You: Yes it is tough. [Focusing on an area of agreement—agreeing in part]

Generating Alternatives

You: What could you do about your smoking? [Asking for specifics—focusing on responsibility for decisions.]
John: I don't know.
You: So . . . you'd like to give up smoking, or cut down maybe, but you feel you can't. [Reflecting.]
John: Well, that's right. Really, it's a matter of just quitting, you just have to quit—not smoke any cigarettes.

Asking for a Decision

You: So you've not really decided to quit and then quit. [Reflecting.]

The basic approach here is to reflect what is said in a way that emphasizes John's responsibility for his own behavior and the difficult but possible change in behavior that he needs to make if he really wants to change. Of course if he doesn't really want to give up smoking, you are wasting your time, since you are not going to be effective until John wants to change.

If at some point you go beyond what John is willing to consider, back off (see Strategy 5). Avoid defending yourself if the other person attacks. John has a right to think what he wants. You are there to help, if you can, not to convince John that he has the wrong idea about you.

There is no need to agree on a solution in this situation. John may have gone as far as he is willing to go in this discussion. The problem belongs to John and you are there to help, not to try to force a solution.

EXAMPLE 2: GETTING "HIRED" TO PROVIDE EXPERTISE BY CONFRONTING

It is important to know the difference between a sentence that puts the other person at ease and invites further conversation and a sentence that has similar wording, but that puts the other person on the defensive. In the following dialogue, Frank, feeling under stress, begins talking about wanting to be more relaxed. A friend offers to help Frank, but is careful to get "hired" first.

Identifying Specifics of the Problem

Frank: I'm really nervous about this interview. I'm not very confident in an interview.

Helper: It's difficult for you to be relaxed. . . . [Reflective listening; drawing implications; said as a simple statement rather than an evaluation.]

Frank: I try to be relaxed, but I just get really nervous.

Helper: Trying to relax doesn't work. [Reflecting John's statement.]

Frank: Right.

Helper: The harder you try to relax the more nervous you get. [Reflecting; drawing implications.]

Comment: This is a hypothesis; the helper is going beyond what Frank has actually said, but he is not evaluating.

Frank: I never thought of it that way, but you are probably right.

Helper: Good. I wasn't sure if that was what you meant. I'm understanding the situation a little better. [I-statement.]

Frank: Well, really then, what it boils down to is that the harder I try to relax, the more nervous I get.

Helper: So the problem or part of it at least, is concentrating so hard on staying relaxed. [Reflecting previous statement; drawing implications.]

Frank: Yeah!

Comment: The helper can't solve John's problem for him, but by helping Frank focus on the situation and his own behavior instead of giving him advice, he has helped Frank understand the problem better.

Asking For A Decision

Helper: (Continuing where conversation left off from above.) Would you like to go into this any deeper? (Inviting further discussion.) I have some expertise in this area and might be able to help if you wish. [I-statement—saying what you're willing to do.]

Frank: Sure, why not?

Helper: I can show you several techniques that are often effective in relaxing. [I-statement—saying what you're willing to do.]
Frank: Go ahead!
Helper: First one. Stand up. O.K. Now... (etc.).

The helper can now proceed to teach Frank what he knows. Notice however that while the helper is sharing his expertise, he is not telling Frank what he should do; he is making what he knows available to Frank without depriving Frank of the responsibility to solve his own problem. Also, Frank makes sure to get hired first, before he does any teaching or shares his expertise. It would have been a mistake, for example, for Frank to start showing the helper some techniques for relaxing immediately after the helper says that he is nervous.

EXAMPLE 3: ENCOURAGING VALUE JUDGMENTS

One of the steps in encouraging others to accept responsibility for their actions is getting them to make value judgments about their actions. In the following example a listener works with a teenager in an attempt not to show the teenager that she is wrong, but to get her to look at what she is doing and whether or not she's helping the situation.

Identifying Specifics of the Problem

Teenager: I can't stand my parents. They're always bugging me. Telling me what to do. Don't do this, don't do that....
Listener: Uh huh... What do you do then?.... [Asking for specifics of behavior.]
Teenager: I just agree with everything they say!
Listener: I'll bet that drives them crazy! [Reflecting; drawing implications without using a judgmental tone of voice.]
Teenager: (Smiles in recognition.) It sure does!

Comment: By entering into the teenager's reality, the listener in this situation is able to establish rapport, and also to indirectly point out the payoff for agreeing with the parents (it drives them crazy). Of course this (it drives

them crazy) is only a guess, but it allows the adult quickly to get at what is really going on in the situation between teenager and parents.
Continuing:

Listener: You enjoy defeating them. (Not said as an accusation.) You are very successful at this. [Reflecting implications.]
Teenager: Yeah... I suppose that's true.
Listener: I can understand that. When you're in a power struggle with someone, it can feel good to defeat them. [Reflecting implications.]
Teenager: Yeah, that's right.

Getting a Value Judgment

Listener: Does that make things better or worse? [Focusing on consequences; asked in a hypothetical way, not a judgmental way.]
Teenager: It just makes them mad (smiles).
Listener: That's right. You show them you can defeat them. [Reflecting implications.]
Teenager: Uh huh. I suppose so.
Listener: You may not have thought about it that way before.
Teenager: (Silence)
Listener: Is defeating them helping you get what you want?
Teenager: Well, sure... they can't push me around.
Listener: Right, but in the long run, are things the way you would like? [Focusing on consequences.]
Teenager: I suppose not....

Given a nonjudgmental atmosphere, questions about consequences and value judgments encourage others to think through situations. Once you make a judgment, that judgment is communicated to the other person in subtle ways—tone of voice, body posture, choice of words. When this happens, the other person feels "I'm not understood" and tends to resist.

This example does not show a solution (that might take an hour session or many sessions), but a way of working. There are few "quick fix" techniques that you can use to change others; what you can do is find a way of working with others that leads to problem solving.

EXAMPLE 4:
GIVING SUPPORT THROUGH NONREASSURANCE

Many people feel that in order to be effective, they must not leave others feeling uneasy or uncertain. Help is supposed to leave people feeling good. In the following dialogue, a boss encourages an employee to accept more responsibility by refusing to make the employee's decisions for her. The boss does not attempt to solve the problem for her, but encourages her to accept responsibility for her decisions by refusing to give unnecessary reassurance. Constant reassurance will only undermine her self-confidence in her own ability to make decisions.

Employee: Is this all right? I'm not sure I've done this the way you want.

Identifying Specifics of the Problem

Supervisor: What is it you have a question about? [Asking for specifics.]

Comment: Note that this question leaves the employee with responsibility for saying what is O.K. and what is not O.K.

Employee: Well, take a look at this. I'm not sure if this is the best way for us to go.
Supervisor: O.K., what would you suggest we do about it? [Asking for specifics—focusing on responsibility.]
Employee: I'm not sure.
Supervisor: You're not sure—that sounds like you have a few ideas. [Reflecting—summarizing, drawing implication of statement to encourage employee to accept responsibility.]
Employee: Well, yes, I thought we could use another approach more efficiently, but I haven't worked it up because I wasn't sure if I should.

Getting a Value Judgment

Supervisor: You think an alternate approach is worth looking at. [Reflecting—encouraging employee to accept responsibility for making a decision about the worth of the alternative approach.]
Employee: Well, yes, it might.

Asking for a Decision

Supervisor: O.K. Would it be a problem for you to work on it?
Employee: Not at all.
Supervisor: Fine. Go ahead and work up whatever alternative plans you have and then we'll go from there. [Accepting responsibility for Mary to go ahead—giving her permission to follow her own ideas.]
Employee: O.K. Fine. I'll get back to you when it's ready.

EXAMPLE 5:
THINKING THROUGH
SELF-DEFEATING ATTITUDES

Helping others to think through attitudes and feelings can be useful in encouraging them to accept responsibility. The following example concerns helping a student confront a problem of feeling that he is a failure. The approach is based on Ellis (1975).

Identifying Specifics
of the Problem

Client: I'm not sure if I can succeed. I've never taken much responsibility before; now I may be taking on more than I can handle.
Helper: You're unsure... [Reflecting feelings.]
Client: Yeah, I just don't know.

Helper: You feel somewhat afraid. [Reflecting feelings.]
Client: I worry about failing... I feel like I can only fail.

Getting a Value Judgment

Helper: What does that do to you? [Asking for specifics.]

Comment: Note that helper does not say "Why do you feel that way?" as that would focus on causes rather than consequences and would very likely produce a defensive reaction.

Client: I suppose I'm setting myself up to fail.
Helper: That's probably right.
Client: I see I can't do very well if I think like that.

The helper is confirming what client has said. He assists the client in understanding the need to stop setting himself up to fail. The helper is saying, "Yes, this is a probable consequence!" The helper needs to be careful not to assume a judgmental attitude that conveys the message, "Yes, you will fail if you don't change—so you had better change."

The difference between giving information and imposing a judgment is often difficult to see, but is critical in being effective. I remember a severely depressed adolescent whose parents were constantly telling him to get out and say hello to people, make friends, be active, and so on. My job was especially difficult because they were right in thinking that unless he changed his behavior, he would not get better. However the methods they used only made him feel guilty and inadequate because he didn't do these things. Part of my task was to help him think through his situation so that he would come to see that he needed to take some risks and talk to people, become involved in activities, and so on. This task was made much more difficult, however, by the discouragement he felt from hearing his "positive-thinking" parents. Anything I might say that sounded like his parents would be rejected, yet I had to help him see on his own the necessity of some of the things they were suggesting.

People who use "positive" thinking may be correct in assuming that a self-defeating attitude may hinder problem solving, but their methods are likely to be ineffective.

EXAMPLE 6:
HELPING OTHERS TO CONFRONT THEIR OWN IMAGE-CENTERED CRITICISM

People who criticize themselves, put themselves down, or otherwise tell themselves that they are stupid, no good, bad, or worthless discourage themselves from acting effectively (Martin, 1980).

By asking problem-centered questions and by then following up on the logical connection between the problem and the person's self-defeating language, you can help others become aware of, and then change, self-defeating patterns of behavior.

The following dialogue is based on the rational-emotive approach (Ellis, 1971, 1977; Ellis & Harper, 1975) to help others question their own self-defeating language. It is a confrontive approach and is unlikely to be effective unless the helper has been "hired" to help.

Identifying Specifics of the Problem

Client: I'm stupid. I can't do anything right!
Listener: You look frustrated. [Reflecting nonverbal behavior.]
Client: I just feel like a failure.
Listener: What is it that makes you feel like a failure? [Asking for specifics.]
Client: Oh, everything!
Listener: Uh huh. . . . What is it right now that you feel upset about? [Focusing on specifics of immediate problem.]
Client: Oh, everything!
Listener: Can you give an example? [Asking for specifics.]
Client: I failed my math test.
Listener: You failed a math test. . . . [Reflecting content; repetition of a key phrase.]
Client: Yes.
Listener: (Silence; nods head.) [Responding nonverbally with attentive silence.]

Comment: The counselor isn't helping the student cope with the problem of passing the course. Until the student copes with this attitude toward himself, the student is unlikely to take a problem-solving approach to his situation.

Client: I'm a failure!

Getting a Value Judgment

Listener: How does failing one test make you a failure? [Asking for specifics.]
Client: Well, because I feel like a failure.
Listener: That's right, you feel like a failure; but does failing this test in reality make you a total failure? [Challenging mistaken logic by asking for the logical connection.]
Client: No, of course not.
Listener: Right. You feel like a failure because you are telling yourself "I'm a failure."
Client: I am?
Listener: Those were your words when you came in here. [Reflecting.]
Client: You're right. But how does that help? I still failed the test.

Asking for a Decision

Listener: True; you failed the test. You can't change that. You can do something about what you're telling yourself.
Client: What do you mean?
Listener: What if you consciously said to yourself: I failed the test, that does not make me a total failure, though I do feel disappointed.
Client: O.K. You're right. So I'm not a total failure. How does that help me?
Listener: Well, for one thing, now we can talk about what you can do about preparing for the next test, starting today. You don't accomplish anything when you feel depressed as a result of telling yourself you're a failure.
Client: I understand. Feeling bad doesn't help.
Listener: Exactly. Now, what can you do to prepare for the next test? [Asking for specifics.]

The danger with using this approach is that explaining and using logic can easily hinder problem solving if you have not been "hired" to help the client in this way. Unless your relationship with the person makes this approach appropriate, *reflecting* may be a better option. In this situation, using a confrontive approach is working.

EXAMPLE 7:
HELPING OTHERS CHALLENGE
THEIR CRITICISM OF OTHERS

Some people avoid responsibility for problems by blaming others (or circumstances or the world). A client blames his depression on his parents; a student blames her poor work on a teacher; a counselor blames his burnout on his clients; and so on. By using problem-centered questions, you can encourage others to examine the rationality of their blaming and criticizing others (a first step toward a more problem-centered approach). The techniques presented here were developed by Albert Ellis (1971, 1977).

Identifying Specifics of the Problem

Mary: My parents don't care whether I go to college or not.
Listener: Your parents don't care and that really bothers you. [Reflecting feelings about the situation.]

Comment: The listener's statement puts into words what the client implies by his tone of voice without actually saying so.

Mary: That's right. I want to go, though. But what's the use, they don't care.
Listener: So you are discouraged about going because of your parents' negative attitude. [Reflecting feelings; summarizing.]
Mary: Yeah...

Getting a Value Judgment

Listener: O.K. You feel discouraged about your parents' attitude. [Reflecting feelings.] But how does that prevent you from going ahead and making plans to go anyway? [Focusing on specific causes.]

Mary: I don't know. It just does.
Listener: Yes, but does it actually *prevent* you from going ahead with your plans to go to college? [Challenging mistaken logic.]
Mary: I suppose not. I don't see how it would do any good, but I could go ahead and apply. Maybe I could get a loan or a scholarship or something, though I don't see much chance.

Generating Alternatives

Listener: O.K., then, do you want to talk about the possibilities? [Inviting discussion.]
Mary: Yeah, why not?
Listener: O.K. Tell me more about what you want to do. [Inviting discussion.]

In this dialogue, the helper actively questions the mistaken (illogical) ideas of the client. The helper begins by reflecting and then encourages the client to question blaming others.

The helper doesn't try to convince the client that blaming others is wrong or bad, but that what others do (or have done) doesn't prevent her from concentrating on the problem at hand and what can be done about it.

What if Alternatives Are Limited?

Problems having to do with relationships, money, the meaning of one's life, illness, and death often have no solution other than to learn to deal with them. What gives people a sense of power over their lives is not that they can control things, but that they can continue to think and feel and act and not be paralyzed by the problems that face them. When others come to you with problems and situations that cannot be resolved, sometimes you can help by encouraging them to focus on what they can do. The techniques in this chapter can be useful even when no resolution is possible.

When people understand that they can act, no matter how desperate their situation, they no longer feel powerless. People sometimes feel caught in the bind of trying to cope with situations that are not of their own making. It is easy to blame the situation, an institution, or even the society, but this does nothing to increase the power of the people you are working with. Conditions beyond their (or your) control may be responsible for their situation, but they need to focus on what they can do. I have worked with children who are very much victims of situations over which they (and I) had no control. Blaming or pitying would have done nothing to help them cope with their situations.

If you work with people who seem unwilling to do anything for themselves, despite your best efforts, it's easy to blame them for the situation in which they find themselves. "If they would try . . ." "If they would only look for a job . . ." And so on. Blaming the individual does nothing to increase his power to act; far from motivating him, it only tends to evoke resentment, self-blame, and guilt.

A Note of Caution

The techniques discussed in this chapter may generate conflict if they sound like accusations. Questions of any kind may put others on the defensive, resulting only in withdrawal or counter-attack. These techniques are confrontive, however you use them. Correctly used, they will encourage the person you are working with to focus on specifics of problem situations and the specifics of what he can do about them.

Basic Principle

> *Solving problems requires focusing on specific details of the problem and what can be done.*

The essence of encouraging others to accept responsibility is to focus on the present situation and on what the individual can do about it. Questions which focus on specifics tend to encourage others by communicating the assumption that they can make decisions and then act on them. Such questions, however, need to be used with caution and in a noncoercive way.

Confronting others when they have a problem requires finding a way to challenge the other person to examine the problem and accept responsibility for acting without feeling defensive or guilty and without blaming others. Perhaps the key to accomplishing this is the ability to enter into the other person's reality and to help him rethink that reality.

When people think of confronting, too many think in terms of *personal* confrontation: *I* confront *you*. In confronting others when they have the problem, you want to avoid a personal confrontation and help others confront the problem and their responsibility for acting.

GUIDELINES

Encourage others to accept responsibility without accepting blame or feeling guilty. Blame and guilt focus on worthiness of the individual rather than on the problem, and seldom lead to responsible behavior. In many situations, it is only when a person stops blaming himself or feeling guilty that he finds the power to take action.

Encourage concern for consequences. Refusing to choose for others, refusing to blame or induce guilt feelings does not mean pretending that actions don't have consequences. Encourage others to look at their choices in terms of their consequences. People are free to choose their actions, but they are not free to choose the consequences of those actions.

Refuse to choose for others. I will put these comments in terms of my own experience: in a helping relationship I want to let others know that I cannot choose for them, even if they want me to.

Express trust through noninterference. We demonstrate our trust in others' ability to accept responsibility and take action by refusing to interfere with their autonomy, whether or not we agree with their decisions.

Express caring and concern. Refusing to accept responsibility for others' problems does not mean not caring or not being involved. I would argue that the capacity to be involved with others in a constructive way is based on the willingness to feel caring and concern without interfering.

Get hired to help. You want to help others confront their own problems, not to confront them personally. If you don't get "hired," you are inviting conflict.

Listen and reflect. Listening and reflecting are necessary in establishing a climate in which you can confront without creating a personal conflict. Even though Strategy 3 relies primarily on *asking for specifics* (Skill 3), the skills of reflecting and responding nonverbally may be needed.

Back off when necessary. You are not there to solve the problem or to coerce; don't go further than the other person is willing to go. Let the other person accept responsibility for the problem if it is his problem. We will consider confronting others when you have the problem in the next chapter. In essence, the goal in confronting others when they have a problem is the same as the goal of listening and reflecting: to help another person focus on the problem and what he or she can do about it.

SUMMARY

Getting others to accept responsibility and make decisions by asking for specifics is a strategy that allows you to focus on the problem without putting the other person on the defensive. This strategy is usually a four-stage process of (1) identifying the specifics of the problem, (2) getting a value judgment, (3) generating alternatives, and (4) asking for a decision. At each stage, it is important that the person with the problem do the work.

chapter twelve

Strategy 4: Negotiating

Ask for what you want and you may get it. Don't ask, and you're sure not to get it. Ask in the wrong way and you make it too easy for others to turn you down.

Negotiating (Strategy 4), is a combination of asking for what you want and listening to the other person. By asking for what you want clearly and directly, you focus on the problem at hand—in this case your own needs. By listening and reflecting, you find out what the other person wants. By both asking for what you want and listening carefully to the other person, you can often reach a mutually acceptable solution.

When To Use

- You have a problem. (Even if the other person is the cause of the problem, if you are the one affected, you have the problem.)
- You want the other person to make a change that will help solve the problem.
- You are willing to ask for what you want, are prepared to set limits, or both.

137

Goals

- Solve your own problems.
- Maintain cooperative relationship with the other person.

The Strategy

Use Skill 1 (reflecting) and skill 4 (making I-statements) to:

- State the problem and ask for what you want using I-statements.
- Listen and clarify the other person's position using reflecting (as many times as necessary).
- Restate and/or modify your own position using I-statements (as many times as necessary).
- Agree on a solution.

Before looking at examples of the strategy in action, we will take a look at the four subgoals in detail:

Stating the Problem and Asking for What One Wants

Stating the problem and asking for what you want is the essence of Strategy 4. In stating the problem it is important to accept responsibility for the problem as *your* problem—even when the other person is responsible for causing the problem. You may not get what you want, but you will almost certainly not get what you want if you don't ask. An I-statement is often the best way to accomplish this. An I-statement puts the emphasis on the problem, instead of on the other person. Also, you can more easily motivate the other person to cooperate by stating the specific effects of the problem on you and how you feel than by blaming the other person. You also want to avoid an argument about who is right or who is to blame because even if the other person is wrong and even if the other person is causing the problem (from your point of view), you will still be more effective if you focus on your problem rather than on the "wrongness" of the other person.

Some people feel that the polite way to ask for something is by hinting. Hints are often either missed, or when not missed, resented or ignored. Indirect statements tend to imply that the other person is at fault, should know better, should feel guilty, and so on. Indirect statements are often experienced as being manipulative rather than polite.

Listening and Clarifying the Other Person's Position

The secret to negotiating successfully is listening. Through listening you learn what the other person's position is and what he or she wants. Strategies 1, 2, and 3 were concerned with listening to others and helping them to solve their problems and meet their needs. Strategy 4 is no different in that successful negotiating requires listening and helping others meet their needs and solve their problems. All of the skills you have for finding out others' needs and what can be done about them can be used in negotiating.

In particular, you need to let the other person know that you understand his or her viewpoint by reflecting. When the other person is talking about his needs and problems, pay attention. For the time being, forget your own point of view, your own objectives, needs, and disagreements and reflect the other person's concerns. You can come back to your position later. In complex situations in which the other person objects, makes excuses, or acts defensive, reflecting will serve to clarify and calm you both so that you both are aware that you understand each other's position.

Restating or Modifying One's Own Position

In many situations you will need to restate and/or modify what you ask for. Repeated I-statements requesting what you want keeps the discussion on the task and is useful in getting a direct answer from the other person.

If you can't get everything you want, go for what you can get. For example, if the other person refuses to make a decision, ask for a specific time when you can have a decision.

Note that restating your position means restating your problem and your needs, rather than accusing the other person of causing a problem. By stating the problem in terms of your own needs and the tangible effect of the other person's problem on you, you avoid accusations. In many conflicts, each side sees its own position as the right one. By concentrating on your problem, you can accept the legitimacy of the other person's position while still insisting that your problem needs a solution. If in the course of listening to the other person you find that you are willing to modify your original position, make that modification part of your position.

When the other person replies to your restatement or modification of your own position, it is important to listen to and clarify what the other person is saying. As long as you continue to clarify the other person's position and to restate and modify your own, you are moving toward a solution.

Agreeing on a Solution

The final step is agreeing on a solution. You don't both have to like the outcome, although of course, that is preferable. Restate the agreement in specific terms so that you are both clear about what has been agreed upon.

EXAMPLE 1:
CONFRONTING UNACCEPTABLE BEHAVIOR

Let us consider these steps in greater detail, using the example of someone blowing smoke in your face. In the following situation, another person, John, is smoking and you object to the smoke. I have chosen this situation to contrast it with a superficially similar but actually very different situation in which you would like to encourage and help John to give up smoking. Determining who has the problem is important in making decisions about what strategy to use. In this situation, you have the problem. You are the one who is directly affected by John's smoking. This is different from John's problem of smoking as an activity that may be injurious to his health. Your problem is not John's habit of smoking, but rather the fact that the smoke is blowing in your face.

Your objective is to meet your own legitimate needs in this situation. The other person doesn't have to "hire" you, he doesn't even have to like your airing the problem. You may be tempted to avoid dealing with your own problems because you don't want to alienate the other person. In the long run, however, unless you deal with your own needs, the situation will become uncomfortable for both parties and you will be less effective in working with this person than you might otherwise be.

Stating the Problem
and Asking for What One Wants

Helper: John, my eyes are really bothering me because of the smoke, would you move your cigarette, please? [Confronting with a three-part I-message.]

Client: I have a right to smoke and I'll smoke if I please. I don't have to stop smoking just because you tell me.

Listening and Clarifying the Other Person's Position

Helper: That's true you have a right to smoke. [Agreeing; reflecting client's basic point.] ... I'm not questioning your right to smoke, but I do have a problem. I'm allergic to the smoke and I'm having trouble concentrating on our conversation. [Avoiding negative cooperation by agreeing; using an I-statement to restate the problem.]

Agreeing on a Solution

Client: O.K. I can see your point. But I still don't feel like putting my cigarette out.
Helper: That's not necessary; perhaps we could try changing our chairs around. [A possible solution.]
Client: Let's just switch chairs.
Helper: Fine, let's try it. [Solution reached.]

It is easier to be assertive if you decide what you want *before* you confront the other person. Otherwise you may be manipulated into accepting a solution that you don't want and could have avoided. You can always change your mind about what you will accept as you acquire new information. Relying on the other person to make things easy for you is usually a mistake.

EXAMPLE 2:
NAILING DOWN
THE SPECIFICS OF A SOLUTION

Solutions may evaporate if you do not get a commitment on the specifics of how, when, and where the solution will be implemented. Getting specifics does not insure results, but they do make it more likely that an agreement will be carried out within a reasonable amount of time. With few exceptions, most people need and want specific information that will help them fit your requests into their schedule. If you don't get a specific commitment, then you are in a very weak position.

In the following example, the two people involved are a committee member (a university professor) and the committee chairman (also a university professor).

Stating the Problem
and Asking for What One Wants

Bill: I'm working on my part of the report this week. When do you need to see a draft? [Asking for specifics.]

Jack: Well, any time this week is good.

Listening and Clarifying
the Other Person's Position

Bill: Well, O.K. how about by five on Friday?

Jack: Now that I think about it I would like to see it before the end of the week.

Restating or Modifying One's Own Position

Bill: I can send you a rough draft by late tomorrow if you need it. [I-statement, says what he is willing to do.]

Agreeing on a Solution

Jack: Well, really I'd prefer to see the final draft. If you can have it by Friday, that would be fine.

Bill: O.K. Thanks. Bye.

As a committee member, Bill sees his task as helping the committee put out a report. He accepts responsibility for his task without being willing to be taken advantage of. By putting the chairman on the spot in a nonthreatening way, he clarifies the situation and negotiates a mutually acceptable course of action. The confronting done here is of a very minor order, yet neglecting to work out a series of minor problems easily leads to a stressful situation in which an individual has trouble helping others because he or she isn't meeting his or her own needs.

EXAMPLE 3: SETTING LIMITS

In any relationship, whether job-related or personal, there are times when you need to set limits. Though problems of setting limits arise even in well-defined relationships, the less defined a relationship, the more likely it is that problems of establishing limits will arise. A job relationship between a supervisor and a factory worker is usually well-defined. The relationship between a counselor and client is less well-defined. The helping relationship that exists between parent and child is very fluid and is continually renegotiated.

In the following example an art teacher, teaching a ceramics course in summer school, offered to help three girls between the ages of eight and ten who wanted to work in a ceramics lab with him while he was working on projects. He showed them how to use the clay. Their interest was intense and they were soon following him around when they saw him go over to the ceramics studio. After much thought, the artist approached the girls the next time he saw them:*

Stating the Problem and Asking for What One Wants

Adult: Girls, I have a problem concerning your being in the lab when I'm working. I feel frustrated when I have to continually answer your questions and supply you with tools and equipment. This takes valuable time and my concentration on my work suffers when I'm interrupted. [I-statements—accepting ownership of the problem.]

Girl 1: You don't want us around any more?

Adult: Well not when I'm working on my ceramic pieces. I need a lot of steady concentration. [I-statement—states needs honestly.]

Girl 2: Gee we like to come over and work with clay. It's fun! Besides there's nothing to do over at the apartments.

*Dialogue supplied by Joel Franken; used with permission.

Adult: I know it's fun to work in clay. [Agreeing.] But I'd rather you would not work in the lab when I'm there. [I-statement; owns problem; restates needs.]

Girl 2: Is there any time we can work in the same lab or are you kicking us out for good?

Restating or Modifying One's Own Position

Adult: No, I think there are certain times you could come over. What are some of the other times we could work out? Do you have any suggestions? [Asking for specifics.]

Girl 1: Are there any times you're over here that you're not concentrating a lot on your work?

Comment: This is interesting in that this girl has responded to the artist's approach with a mature problem-solving approach that models his.

Adult: Yes, there are the times when I'm firing the kiln; you could come over when I'm spending time doing that. Or you could come when I'm mixing clay. Both take a couple of hours and that would be enough time for you to work. Does that seem fair, to limit you to working when I'm doing those other two jobs? [Says what he is willing to do.]

Girl 2: It sounds better than not being able to come at all. I like the sound of that plan.

Girl 1: Me too.

Girl 2: How will we know if you're mixing or firing the oven or kiln? Whatever? [Problem-centered questions.]

Adult: When you see me walking over to the lab, you can ask me if today is a good day to work in the lab. I'll tell you yes or no. Okay? [I-statements—says what he is willing to do.]

Girl 1: Sounds good to me.

Girl 2: Me too.

Agreeing on a Solution

Adult: Well, that sounds like a plan we can all live with. [Reflecting—summarizes decision.] If you don't get over for a long time, we can take a look at a different plan to get you some clay time. Okay?

Girl 1:   Thanks a lot. See you.
Girl 2:   Bye.

The artist states, "I usually handled situations like this in a very authoritarian way or not at all. I felt good that I was not letting three small kids dictate to me in my lab area, but still maintain a two-way respect and admiration." Note that in this example there was no obvious statement in which the adult was clarifying what the girls were saying; in this case it was not necessary.

EXAMPLE 4: USING THE SKILLS TO NEGOTIATE ON THE JOB

Inviting problem-centered criticism can also be useful in obtaining information you need to make decisions and prepare for future negotiations.

In the following situation, an employee feels that she is doing an effective job and should have a promotion. She goes to see her administrator in an attempt to get more specific information by asking for problem-centered criticism.

Stating the Problem and Asking for What One Wants

Employee: I am very concerned that I didn't get a promotion this period and I came in to talk about what I could do in the coming period to merit a raise.

Administrator: We are pleased with your work, but we couldn't promote everyone we would have liked to.

Listening and Clarifying the Other Person's Position

Employee: I see. Is there anything I need to be doing which I haven't done, in order to get a promotion? [Asking for specific problem-centered criticism.]

Administrator: No you are doing fine. Just continue as you are.

Restating or Modifying One's Own Position

Employee: I would like to be recommended, then, for promotion.
Administrator: You can reapply and you will be reconsidered at our next scheduled promotion date.

Agreeing on a Solution

Employee: I'll do that.

At first glance, not much has been accomplished. You have not gotten much. Or have you? I remember finding myself in a situation like this where there would have been little point in arguing about a decision that was already made. I could have argued, but I would not have gotten anywhere.

By asking what I could do, two things were accomplished. First, if there had been something I could work on, I would have known about it and would be able to present evidence that I had accomplished it. Second, by getting specific information about what I needed to do in advance, I forestalled the possibility of being told next time, "You could do X better." So, without anything being actually said, once I was told to continue as I was, the administrator was going to be in a tough spot to explain next time why I didn't get a promotion.

Getting the administrator to be specific didn't put me on the defensive; it would have put him on the defensive if he didn't follow through on his statements. Whether I actually got the promotion at a later time (in fact I did) is not relevant. The point is that by asking for specific information about my own performance, I was acquiring information that I could then use to change my own performance or to document that I had already met the criteria. Either way, soliciting problem-centered criticism would have been useful.

In emphasizing the cooperative, problem-solving possibilities of this approach, you avoid appearing self-centered, and in the long run are more likely to be able to work effectively with others. When you approach a situation with the attitude of "How can I get my way?" you can easily become embroiled in a win-or-lose struggle. Be assertive, but avoid trying to get the best of the other person. Once you get into a power struggle with someone, you may either win or lose, but in either case, your ability to work effectively with the other person is lessened.

MISTAKEN REASONS WHY PEOPLE AVOID CONFRONTATION

Plausible but mistaken reasoning is often behind a reluctance to say what needs to be said. There is some truth to each of the following statements, but the sentiments they express are often used to rationalize avoidance of a confrontation.

The other person might not like what you say (and that would be awful). It is true enough that the other person might not like what you say, but why is that awful? The other person may dislike what you say without disliking you. Although it may be preferable for people to like you, even if they should dislike you, you can still be effective when you negotiate with them.

What you have to say is unpleasant (and therefore you shouldn't say it). If there weren't a problem, there would be no need for using Strategy 4 to confront the other person. You are not creating what is unpleasant, you are bringing it out in the open. Your bringing up a problem that is unpleasant does not require you to sound or act unpleasant. Unfortunately, many people avoid negotiating when they have a problem in the belief that it is easier not to. The relevant question you need to answer is whether avoiding discussion of a problem is easier in the long run. In many cases, what seems easier in the short run creates frustration and resentment and a feeling of powerlessness which make working relationships impossible.

You might be rejected. Rejection is possible, but happens far less than many people anticipate. Some people may walk out if you don't let yourself be manipulated. In most situations, however, as long as you are problem-centered and do not attack the other person, you will not be rejected.

It is easier to drop hints. Hinting and being indirect may be easier in the short run, but it is seldom effective. Dropping hints lends itself to playing games, and others will respond by also playing games, e.g., by pretending not to understand.

The consequences will be unpleasant. The rationalization I hear most often for people not saying what needs to be said is "I might get into trouble," or "I might get fired," especially if the person they need to confront is a superior. While people may be fired for aggressive behavior, very few are ever fired for saying what needs to be said in a calm, rational tone of voice that avoids attacking or threatening the other person. There are people who "cannot stand" being confronted—that is they manipulate other people into submission by throwing tantrums when confronted. The next chapter provides a strategy for coping with such people.

It's not your style. There is no one style to be used in confronting. The quiet, shy, gentle person may be as effective as more talkative people. Quiet, mild-mannered individuals may not generate in the other person the resistance that more talkative people sometimes do.

You are uncomfortable. At first many people feel uncomfortable when they begin to change their behavior. "It's not me, I'm not like that, it's not my style, I could never do that," etc., are common excuses people use to avoid changing their behavior. Although it is desirable to feel comfortable with the techniques you use, it is sometimes more important to change your behavior than to feel comfortable. As in learning any skill, the more skillful you become, the more comfortable you will be using that skill. Take action. You don't always have to feel comfortable.

You will discourage the other person. It is very common for people to feel that they don't want to upset others. However, confronting a problem, no matter how severe, is almost always more encouraging than trying to avoid it.

Confrontations are unnecessary in a good relationship. Inability to confront when needed is generally a sign of a problem relationship. Confrontations in an ongoing relationship are sometimes necessary to resolve problems and maintain the relationship.

GUIDELINES

Use language which can be understood by the other person. Simple sentences (subject, verb, object) are often the best. Overly complex sentences don't make the point.

Be direct. Avoid unnecessary qualifying, disclaiming, apologizing, and beating around the bush.

Speak honestly about the situation. Don't try to put things in a better light than they are; on the other hand, don't dramatize.

Be prepared. Research your position. Know what is a reasonable request. Know what other people have been able to get in similar circumstances. Know your limits and what you are willing to settle for.

Be polite but persistent. Don't immediately give up when given a *no* answer. Explore the situation further if possible. The other person may give you a flat *no* on what you have asked for and yet be willing to give you part of what you want, or something else that is just as good.

SUMMARY

The essence of negotiating with others when you have a problem is using I-statements to ask for what you want instead of making "you" statements that put the other person on the defensive. Listening and reflecting are also important because they allow you to understand and respond to the other person, and they open the way for finding a mutually acceptable solution.

chapter thirteen

Strategy 5: Staying problem centered when attacked

No matter how effective you are, there are times when others will try to get you into a power struggle. When this happens, acting defensively encourages an unproductive power struggle. Strategy 5 allows you to stay calm and avoid defensive behavior.

When to Use

- You have the problem of someone attacking you or attempting to engage you in a power struggle. You don't have to like or agree with the attack; you do need to cope with it.
- You want to turn the attack into a problem-centered discussion.
- You are willing to discuss the problem but not to engage in a fight or give in.

Goals

- Stay problem-centered when under attack.
- Avoid acting defensively under attack.
- Get discussion onto the problem instead of on you.

The Strategy

Use the skills as necessary to:

- Respond nonverbally until the other person finishes what he has to say.
- Reflect the other person's concerns.
- Focus on areas of agreement.
- Ask for specifics of legitimate problems or criticisms.
- Use I-statements to set limits without fighting or giving in.

There is no set sequence of what to do in coping with attacks. Use the skills as you need them, moving on to one of the other four strategies as soon as possible.

EXAMPLE 1:
AVOIDING DEFENSIVENESS
BY REFLECTING

Reflecting is often an excellent way of changing the focus back to the person who is attempting to engage you in a nonproductive discussion. Reflecting allows you to change the focus from the challenged to the challenger without either agreeing or disagreeing:

Wanting Help:	You should be willing to tell me what's the best thing to do; you're supposed to be the expert. [Resisting accepting responsibility for making decisions by attempting to put the listener on the defensive.]
Listener:	You would like me to tell you what to do.... [Avoiding a power struggle by reflecting.]
Wanting Help:	You're not helping me much; you are not helping me feel any different.
Listener:	You don't notice any change; you don't feel any different. [Reflecting; avoiding a power struggle.]

Complaints about unsatisfactory service are a classic problem for any group of people who supply a service, from counselors and educators to sales and service representatives in business and industry. By reflecting Wanting Help's statements, Listener changes the focus from his answer back to Wanting Help's question.

Dealing with complainers without discouraging them can be difficult. "You don't notice any change; you don't feel any different" focuses not on the fact of whether or not the client is better, but on his observations and feelings. The listener's response is not simply a reflecting statement; it creates a change of focus from the objective question of whether the client is improving to the subjective (and no less real) question of his view of things.

You may sometimes find yourself being drawn into a power struggle because you don't want the other person to become discouraged. When this happens, reflecting feelings allows you to focus on the other person's concerns instead of your own. Reflecting is also useful in focusing on the other person's true concerns rather than toward stated concerns. In the example above, the client's stated concerns toward the help he is getting ("You're not helping me . . .") avoids the real issue: the speaker feels frustrated because he doesn't notice any change in himself. The listener recognizes this and responds to the underlying issue.

EXAMPLE 2:
REFLECTING A VIEWPOINT WITHOUT ACTING ON IT

There may be times when you want to recognize the existence and legitimacy of another person's viewpoint without acting on it.

Group Member: I think we should change our meeting time; we aren't getting enough done. [Challenging tone of voice.]

Leader: There is a suggestion that we change our meeting time. Are there any other suggestions? [Reflecting; avoiding defensive behavior.]

When all suggestions have been made, the leader can then represent these as options available to the group. By using reflecting in this way, a leader can distance options from the individuals who made them, thus helping to minimize potential interpersonal conflict over whose ideas are accepted and whose ideas are rejected.

EXAMPLE 3:
RESPONDING TO LEGITIMATE COMPLAINTS

When someone comes to you with a legitimate complaint presented in an aggressive way, it may be important to deal with that complaint without destroying your ability to work with that person in the future. One of the problems in dealing with complaints is that it is difficult to remain calm and rational when the other person is unreasonable. In the following example, Susan is understandably angry, but instead of expressing that anger by saying how she feels, she resorts to blaming. Dale responds to several legitimate complaints by accepting responsibility for his own actions without becoming defensive.

Susan: You said you would be here at one o'clock.
Dale: You're right. I am late. [Agreeing, I-statement—accepting responsibility for actions.]
Susan: Well, do you remember what I told you last week?
Dale: I don't recall. [I-statement—accepting responsibility.] What can I do for you? [Asking for specifics.]
Susan: How can we work together when you can't even remember what we talked about last time? Can't you even remember what I said a week ago?
Dale: I can see that it really bothers you. [Reflecting feelings; focus on Susan.]
Susan: Yes, it makes me feel like I'm just another face coming in here to talk.
Dale: You're not sure whether I really listen. [Reflective listening.]
Susan: Yeah, that's the impression I get.
Dale: I'll do my best to listen. [I-statement.] What is it you wanted to talk about? [Asking for specifics.]
Susan: Well, it's about . . . (continues).

Dale accepts responsibility for forgetting (never mind that he should have made notes, that he should have been prepared), and then moves on to a problem-centered question.

EXAMPLE 4:
COPING WITH ANGER
AND FRUSTRATION DIRECTED AT YOU

You can use the skills to cope with anger and frustration without either acting defensive or coercive. If you have ever tried to help someone only to find your efforts resented, you may identify with the tutor in the following situation:

Person In Need: You're supposed to be helping me with my work but I'm not doing any better than I was when we started. [Hostile tone of voice directed at tutor.]

Tutor: Your work hasn't gotten any better. [Reflecting; avoiding a power struggle.]

Person In Need: You ought to be sorry. You haven't been much help.

Tutor: It's frustrating not to make any progress. [Reflecting feelings.]

Comment: Explaining or defending in this situation is likely to sound defensive.

Person In Need: Well, what are you going to do about it? [Attempting to reverse the situation by placing the responsibility on helper.]

Tutor: What do you want to do? [Asking for specifics—focusing on Person in Need's responsibility; ignoring provocation.]

Person In Need: Well, if you would go over everything with me, I would do better.

Tutor: I'm willing to check your work and answer any questions you have after you have worked on the assignment. [I-statement; says what she is willing to do.]

Person In Need: That's not going to work. That's what we've been doing. You just aren't willing to really work with me.

Comment: Setting limits may require restating one's own position, continuing to reflect the other person's position and feelings, and finally to change those limits when the situation warrants.

Tutor: I'm willing to work with you: I'm not willing to do the work for you. [I-statement says when she is willing.]

Person In Need: Well, I don't know.

Tutor: You seem more worried about this than you were a week ago. [Reflecting feelings.]

Person In Need: Well, I have good reason to be.

Tutor: You see more need for concern. [Reflecting.]

Person In Need: If I don't get more done, I'm finished.

Tutor: There's more pressure now. [Reflecting.]

Person In Need: Yeah, that's it. I realize you can't help me if I don't put in the effort.

Tutor: Would you be willing to set up a specific schedule where we can work out what you will do and how I'll help? [Asking for specifics.]

Person In Need: That sounds like a good idea. Let's go ahead and do that.

In this situation, it would be very easy for the tutor to feel, *Why should I put up with this? What have I done to deserve this?* and then respond by feeling irritated and then being defensive or aggressive. By refusing to be manipulated into doing more, the helper lets the Person In Need know that he will have to take responsibility for his work. The helper is teaching the Person In Need how she wants to be treated by not responding to his attempts to manipulate her. Once the Person In Need realizes that he is not getting anywhere by trying to pin responsibility for his problems on the Tutor, he is more cooperative.

EXAMPLE 5:
COPING WITH RESISTANCE

People sometimes ask for help and then resist it by talking about all their reservations and bad experiences in a hostile way. When someone asks for help, but doesn't want to talk about the problem, one approach is to listen, agree where appropriate, and give information about what you are willing to do.

Situation: A parent comes in to see a helping professional to ask for help for her daughter.

Client:	I am not sure I really want to be here. My husband didn't want me to come. In my family there's a rule, everything should stay in the family, you take care of things yourself. [Client feels defensive and reacts by attacking.]
Helper:	Your family would prefer you not come. [Reflecting content—paraphrasing.]
Client:	They sure do. For one thing, I can't really afford this. If you people want to help your fellow man, how come you charge so much?
Helper:	It can seem expensive. [Focusing on area of agreement.]
Client:	Besides, what do you know about the situation? Are you married by the way?
Helper:	Yes, I am married.
Client:	Do you have any children?
Helper:	We have a baby girl.
Client:	Well your children aren't even in school. How can you tell me what I should do?
Helper:	You're concerned I might not be any help. [Reflecting implications and avoiding a power struggle.]

Comment: Instead of trying to convince the client that she is qualified to help, the helper reflects back the basic concerns of the client about getting help. If a client really wants to know your qualifications (presuming that you have not established this before you begin to help) then, of course presenting your qualifications is the ethical and appropriate thing to do. However, in many situations, a client may want help and yet be suspicious about the help that is available.

Client: Well, I'm sure you're very educated and everything, it's just that ...

Helper: It's hard to take a chance when you don't even know me. [Reflecting feelings and implications.]

Client: Well, I don't mean to attack you ...

Helper: Would you like to tell me what brings you here? [Inviting client to talk about her problem; avoiding a power struggle by ignoring client's remark.]

In this situation, the helper can't win if she tries to defend herself. No matter what her qualifications and experience, if she defends herself, the client will find something else to find fault with. Reflective listening is often not appropriate when you are asked a direct question, especially regarding your own experience. State your experience if you are qualified to help. If the problem is beyond what you can deal with, refer the person to someone who can.

EXAMPLE 6:
CONFRONTATIONS DESIGNED TO DEFEAT YOU

Others may sometimes attack in an attempt to defeat you. Someone may want help and yet feel afraid of asking for it. Defeating the person who could help is one way to avoid facing a problem while maintaining the fiction that one would change if only it weren't for the helper. The following situation involves a parent who wants help for her son, Ralph.

Parent: Maybe you can do something with Ralph. I've given up. I've tried everything I can, but he just doesn't respond. [Attempt to put responsibility on the helper.]

Helper: Uh huh. [Responding nonverbally—listening cues.]

Parent: He just won't cooperate. Everything I want him to do, he does the opposite.

Helper: He likes to defeat you. [Reflecting implication; paraphrasing.]

Parent:	Boy, does he. And he's always into something. Always getting into trouble. Always somewhere he shouldn't be. [Parent goes on like this for five more minutes, complaining, avoiding responsibility, avoiding specifics.]
Helper:	Could you give me an example of the problems you're having? [Asking for specifics.]
Parent:	Oh, gee, I can't think of anything right off. It's just everything. Like he never minds me.
Helper:	O.K. Can you think of a specific situation where he doesn't mind? [Asking for specifics.]
Parent:	Well, I suppose you think I'm not a very good mother that I don't make him mind. What do you think I should do? [Attempting to put helper on the defensive.]
Helper:	I need specific examples so that I can understand the situation better. [I-statement; asking for specifics.]
Parent:	You're the expert. You figure out what's wrong with Ralph. You fix him up so he behaves.
Helper:	Uh huh... Ralph is a real problem. [Reflecting; focusing on an area of agreement by stating facts without contradicting.]

What about moving on to another strategy? There may not be much the helper can do here. If the parent refuses to cooperate by refusing to accept responsibility or by refusing to provide specific information, the helper is in a real bind. If he accepts responsibility for changing Ralph, he's in trouble. If he confronts the parent by telling her that she's not accepting responsibility for change, she becomes angry at the helper for thinking the situation is her fault. The parent is attempting to manipulate the helper so that she can defeat him either by letting him take responsibility for single-handedly changing Ralph, or by leaving in a huff when he suggests she will have to take some responsibility for Ralph. The reflective listening response he gives ("Ralph is a real problem") sidesteps both traps. People who successfully get others to take a position where they can be defeated are often very skillful in playing this game.

EXAMPLE 7:
RESPONDING TO CRITICISM
OF YOUR APPROACH

People may confront you about your use of skills such as those described in this book. The following example shows one way of accepting responsibility for using the skills without being defensive.

Critic:	I feel like you're trying to use psychology on me.
Jane:	I wasn't aware I was doing that [I-statement.] What is it that gives that impression? [Asking for specifics.]
Critic:	Everything I say, you repeat back to me or you ask me a dumb question.
Jane:	I am working at being a better listener. [I-statement—accepting responsibility for actions.]
Critic:	Well, I just feel like I'm some kind of experiment.
Jane:	I wasn't aware I was giving that impression. [I-statement.]
Critic:	Well, you are.
Jane:	Is there anything else that is bothering you? [Focusing on specifics—inviting specific questions.]
Critic:	Well, you never get mad. No matter what I say, you don't react. I could say anything to provoke you and you would just sit there.
Jane:	You would prefer me to get mad. [Reflecting client's attitude.]
Critic:	Well, why don't you? Anyone else would.
Jane:	I don't like being manipulated into getting mad. [I-statement.]
Critic:	I just don't like feeling like you're trying things out on me.
Jane:	I wouldn't like that either. [I-statement.] Shall we go back to this other problem you were going to bring up? [Problem-centered statement.]
Critic:	O.K.

You must decide where it is appropriate to make I-statements (which place the focus on you) and where it is appropriate to use reflective listening (which places the focus on the client).

EXAMPLE 8:
REQUESTS FOR HELP
DISGUISED AS CRITICISM

People who want help but fear rejection or disappointment may go about asking for help in an argumentative way. In the following example, Sue first puts her mother on the defensive and then asks for help. Not a very good strategy, but one that is often used. The mother is tired and unprepared to cope with the demands made by Sue, and she protects herself by using a variety of image-centered responses.

An Example of an Ineffective Response.*

Sue: Where have you been, Mom? I thought you would never get home. [Questioning, image-centered criticism.] I've got something important to ask you. [Implied request for help.]

Mom: [Crossly.] Sue, you know I always have to finish up my lesson plans on Friday after school. I can't ever seem to get them finished during school hours. Sure would be nice to have an hour break every day like the high school teachers. [Defensive response which invites further criticism.]

Sue: Why don't you teach high school? [Questioning.]

Mom: I'm not qualified. Besides, I like teaching younger children. I've told you that before. [Defensive reply; attacking tone of voice.]

Sue: Then stop complaining [Sarcastically. Ordering, unwanted advice.]

Mom: Now listen, young lady . . . [Threatening.]

Sue: Sorry, Mom. I didn't mean to be smart.

Mom: Now what is this important thing you have to ask me that just can't wait? If it's, are we going to the ballgame, the answer is NO. The game is at Bogland; you know that's a bit far. We will try to see the next home game. And no I won't take you back to Waterville to catch the bus. [Mistaken problem ownership.]

Sue: Gee.

Mom: Gee what?

Sue: I haven't even asked you anything yet. I can see I've been wasting my time. Thanks for nothing. [Sue leaves for her room.]

Sue: [Half an hour later, Sue returns.] Mom?

Mom: Yes, little door slammer? [Sarcasm. Blows a chance to start on a new footing.]

A More Effective Approach

In the above example, Sue wants to "hire" Mom, but Mom is suspicious and reacts defensively. They never get to the problem because both use ineffective approaches. In the following transcript, Sue's replies are the same but Mom refuses to be drawn into a defensive position, and, as the following

*Example supplied by a graduate student; used with permission.

dialogue shows, is more effective in getting Sue to talk:

Sue: Where have you been, Mom? I thought you would never get home. I've got something to ask you.
Mom: Yes, I am later today. [Agreeing by stating facts without being defensive.] Sure would be nice to have an hour break like the high school teachers. [Agreeing.]
Sue: Why don't you teach high school?
Mom: That's an idea. [Avoiding a power struggle by agreeing, refusing to argue.]
Sue: You're always complaining.
Mom: I feel put down by that remark. [I-statement.]
Sue: Sorry, Mom. I didn't mean to be smart.
Mom: Now, what is it you need to ask me? [Asking for specifics.]
Sue: Well ... [Goes on to explain problem.]

People tend to respond with ineffective approaches when they think they need to defend themselves. As the dialogue above shows, however, refusing to be drawn into an argument is far more effective in eliminating hostile behavior, and allows you to remain calm.

GUIDELINES

Don't defend yourself. Defending yourself is generally ineffective for two reasons. First, when you defend yourself, you provide the other person with material with which to attack. Second, it is almost impossible to defend yourself without acting defensive, and when you act defensive you put yourself on a lower level than the person you are answering, and this invites the other person to continue the attack.

The difficulty in giving up defending yourself is that it is easy to think, "I should defend myself." The belief that you have to defend yourself is an irrational belief that allows others to involve us in a fight. When we refuse to defend ourselves, the other person can't fight.

One way to avoid acting defensive is to learn to respond to accusatory questions. Questions, especially questions that put you on the defensive, are among the most difficult situations to deal with. Almost any answer you can think of is likely to sound defensive. The important point to realize is that *you don't have to answer a question that is an accusation*. You can respond without answering the question. For example, you can ignore the question and go on to focus on the problem, you can reflect the other person's concerns, or you can agree in whole or in part with what the other person has said. However, as long as you don't try to defend yourself, you can continue responding as an equal and without becoming defensive.

Don't accept blame. By accepting blame, I mean agreeing with personal attacks on you. You can agree that you have made a mistake without admitting that your mistake makes you less worthwhile. Accepting blame is defensive and tends to invite further attacks, while admitting mistakes can be useful in short-circuiting attacks. Blame is image-centered, and agreeing with image-centered criticism tends to encourage further criticism.

Accepting blame implies that you are less worthwhile and should think less well of yourself because of what you have done. Since there is never a rational or legitimate reason for considering ourselves less worthwhile than another person, there is never any reason to accept blame.

Accepting blame and feeling guilty have little or no survival value. They put us in the position of feeling and acting inferior. Once in an inferior position, we are easily manipulated.

Avoid apologizing and offering excuses. Apologizing and offering excuses are defensive behaviors, and they invite manipulation. These behaviors also give an impression of nonassertiveness and incompetence. Apologies containing references to "trying" are especially weak ("I tried ....", "I'll try harder next time ....", etc.) and give the impression of avoiding responsibility.

Avoid placating. Attempting to placate others sometimes seems to be an easy way out of difficult situations, but it invites further manipulation and intimidation by reinforcing these behaviors.

When in a power struggle, don't try to change the other person's mind by arguing. The harder you try to convince others that you are right, the easier you make it for others to draw you into a power struggle. Many people mistakenly feel that if they don't attempt to correct erroneous statements or attacks, that they are agreeing with them. In particular, trying to convince others that their opinion of you is wrong invites a power struggle.

We tend to get into power struggles when we irrationally believe that:

- I should be able to change other people's minds.
- Other people shouldn't act the way they do act.
- It is my job to change others.

When we feel we should be able to change others, we make it possible for them to involve us in power struggles and to then defeat us by refusing to cooperate. The alternative is to use the skills to respond calmly, even when you don't feel calm.

SUMMARY

Never be defensive. Defensive behavior invites further attack and puts you in a one down position. The five skills, particularly the skill of focusing on an area of agreement, can be used to avoid defensiveness while attempting to focus on the problem. Strategy 5 encourages cooperation; where cooperation is not possible, it leaves the door open to future cooperation.

part four

AVOIDING TRAPS

Using effectively the skills and strategies presented in Parts II and III takes practice. Skeptics like to point out that these skills "sound nice" but that in the "real world" they aren't easy to put into practice. I agree. Techniques are only a way of making communication and problem-solving possible. Techniques have no magic in themselves, although for those able to switch from patterns involving frustration and discouragement to patterns which create mutual cooperation and satisfaction, the experience of change sometimes seems magical.

Proficiency in using the skills and strategies is not always sufficient for effectiveness. To choose your response effectively, you need to decide what is your responsibility and what is the other person's responsibility. The skills and strategies won't work if you accept responsibility that belongs to others. The next three chapters look at the problem of responsibility and the traps that result from a false sense of responsibility.

chapter fourteen

The trap of false responsibility

Choosing an appropriate strategy in a given situation depends on your ability to figure out who has the problem, what the other person wants, and then deciding what you are willing to do. Nothing interferes with this process more than a false sense of responsibility. On the other hand, few experiences are more liberating than freeing yourself of a false sense of responsibility.

Our culture encourages us to accept responsibility for others and their problems and to feel anxious or guilty when we don't. Accepting responsibility for problems which belong to others not only doesn't help others, it often interferes with our ability to perceive accurately, think rationally, and act effectively.

Rather than leading to increased caring and sensitivity, accepting responsibility for the problems of others often:

- Leads to feeling upset, miserable, and guilty about the problems of others.
- Induces us to manipulate others in the name of helping them.
- Distorts our perception of a situation by leading us to focus on finding a solution instead of listening and understanding.

If you accept responsibility for others' problems, you relieve them of their sense of responsibility for those problems.

Basic Principle

Accepting responsibility for solving the problems of others teaches them that they don't need to accept responsibility for solving those problems.

The intended effect of accepting responsibility for others is to help them solve their problems. The actual effect of accepting responsibility for solving others' problems is that we teach others to be less powerful and less able to cope. In the short run, this may not matter, but in the long run, we are teaching others to avoid responsibility; we are encouraging them to be dependent on us or on others.

Our culture tends to exalt people who do things *for* others. Fairy godmothers, genies, Superman (and woman), Perry Mason, and Marcus Welby—all present an image of untainted power and goodness that asks for nothing in return. This image, caricature though it is, represents a mistaken assumption that it is always virtuous to do *for* others.

WHY ACCEPTING RESPONSIBILITY FOR OTHERS DOESN'T WORK

Accepting responsibility for the problems of others discourages them from accepting responsibility for their own problems. Attempting to make a decision for someone that only he can make reduces his ability to make decisions and act. It is especially easy to reinforce learned helplessness and irresponsibility in someone who already has difficulty acting on his own. The five-year-old who has trouble with her boots, the handicapped person who is unable to do many things for himself, the retarded person who is slow to make decisions—these people are easily reduced by well-meaning people to a life of dependence and powerlessness.

Accepting responsibility for others' problems often results in stress and anxiety for both you and the other person. You can literally make yourself sick over the problems of others. Symptoms such as tiredness, high blood pressure, anxiety, ulcers, headaches, as well as feelings of frustration or discouragement are common reactions to what seem like overwhelming demands.

Therapists who work with people whose problems include depression, suicide attempts, or problems related to misusing drugs quickly discover that accepting responsibility for solving a client's problem is a luxury that they cannot afford. In dealing with problems that are less severe, we have the luxury of taking on other people's problems as our own. The question is whether we want to. By accepting responsibility for a problem that you cannot solve, you may lose your own ability to avoid discouragement, to listen, to be empathetic, to encourage others, and to help them focus on their own responsibility.

BENEFITS OF NOT ACCEPTING RESPONSIBILITY FOR PROBLEMS THAT BELONG TO OTHERS

Keeping your sanity. Not accepting responsibility for problems that are not yours can help you keep your sanity in situations that would otherwise be highly stressful.

Listening more easily. When you don't feel responsible for solving another's problem, you can listen more easily without feeling the need to advise, question, lecture, and so on.

Being more empathetic. Empathy means understanding how another feels—understanding the other person's hurt, frustration, anger, or discouragement without being hurt, frustrated, angry, or discouraged yourself. By not accepting responsibility for another's problem, you are less likely to become trapped in the same feelings as the person you are trying to help.

Encourage mutual respect. By allowing others the respect and dignity of being responsible for their own problems, you communicate a sense of trust.

Encourage others to focus on their own responsibilities. By not trying to solve others' problems for them, you can help them focus on what they can do.

A Note on "It's Not My Problem"

Not accepting responsibility for the problems of others is not an excuse for indifference. The point of this chapter is that it is only when you do not accept responsibility for solving the problems of others that you are in a position to provide genuine help. The fact that something is not your problem is not an excuse for failure to act responsibly. For example, I am not responsible for what you, the reader, do with the techniques that you take from this book. That is clearly your responsibility. On the other hand, it is my responsibility to protect from misinterpretation all of the ideas that appear here. A second example: I am not responsible for the feelings, decisions, and actions of my students or even my own children. I cannot control them or choose for them or act for them. I am, however, responsible for what I do to teach, encourage, and help them think through problems.

The assumption that we should control or direct others by reason of our superior power, knowledge, or authority can lead to coercion and manipulation that leaves both us and others feeling frustrated and discouraged (Dreikurs 1953, 1958, 1971; Dreikurs, Grunwald, & Pepper, 1971).

IRRATIONAL ARGUMENTS THAT PRESSURE PEOPLE INTO THE TRAP OF FALSE RESPONSIBILITY

One reason we sometimes accept responsibility for others when we and they would be better off if we didn't is that we are pressured by arguments that sound plausible but are irrational. These arguments influence us without our being aware of them; but by becoming consciously aware of them, we can choose to ignore them and refuse to accept responsibility for others or for problems over which you have no control. The following statements are myths that sound true because we have heard them so often; by recognizing them as myths, we can more easily avoid the trap of false responsibility:

Myth: It's your responsibility; it's your job. It is not your job to accept responsibility for the behavior of others; it is your job to do whatever possible to influence others to act responsibly, and to cope with them when they don't act responsibly.

Myth: You are expected to. Other people may expect you to feel responsible for actions or situations over which you have no control, but you don't have to accept these expectations. In such situations you may want to ask yourself:

- Are the expectations placed on me legitimate?
- Can they be fulfilled or are they impossible?
- Do they make sense?

You may feel that you have to accept the expectations of your boss or be fired. However, you are more likely to be evaluated by what you do and the results you achieve than by what you think. Meeting the boss's *performance* expectations doesn't mean you have to accept his or her expectation that you feel responsible for the behavior or problems of others. In fact you are more likely to meet the performance expectations of your job if you don't feel responsible for the behavior or problems of others. Focus on your own behavior and what you can do, rather than feeling responsible for the actions of others.

Myth: If you don't accept responsibility, you don't care. The closer we are to others, the more easily we may fall into the trap of accepting responsibility for their problems. One reason is that it is easy to confuse caring, concern, and even love with feeling responsible (and miserable) for others. This confusion discourages others (especially people with whom we have a close relationship) from developing a sense of responsibility for their own behavior.

Myth: You should feel guilty if you don't. The belief that you should feel guilty if you don't accept responsibility for others' problems is based on myths we have already discussed: It's your responsibility to interfere; if you don't interfere you don't care; if you don't interfere you're not living up to your obligations, to the expectations of others, and so on. The feeling of guilt we may experience when we don't rush in to accept responsibility for others does not come from the rightness or wrongness of our actions but from what we tell ourselves and from mistaken images of effective helping.

When we assume responsibility for solving problems that belong to others, we become concerned with how to get results and easily become trapped into trying to control others. We begin by asking what seem to be perfectly reasonable questions:

- How can I influence her so that she will *want* to do what is best for her?
- What can I do to motivate him?
- How can I make them behave?
- How can I get John to accept responsibility?
- How can I improve their attitude?

Questions like these easily trap us into trying to solve problems that we can't solve by implying that we *should* or *must* be able to control what happens. Once we assume that we *should* or *must* bring about a certain result, this assumption requires us to try to control the situation. We may begin trying to control by using "positive" means such as praising, hinting, and suggesting, and then find ourselves unintentionally and unwillingly drawn into using more coercive means—usually with little result.

Myth: You are more powerful, therefore you should accept responsibility for another's problem. You may not think of yourself as powerful when you work with others, and yet act in ways that suggest that you are trying to control others. Particularly in situations in which you are relatively more powerful than the person you are trying to help, it is easy to encourage powerlessness in the other person. Teachers, employers, supervisors, social workers, counselors, and parents often have relatively more authority and power than their students, employees, supervisors, clients, and children.

Myth: If others are weaker, more ignorant, less capable, less competent, or less experienced, you should accept responsibility for their problem. When we assume that others are weaker or less powerful than they are, we encourage them to act powerless. As soon as you assume that you are superior to others you are going to communicate that assumption in one way or another. At times you may find it difficult to resist the temptation to assume that you know what is right or best for someone else. Even where you may be right in your assumptions, making a decision for another person is a way of taking responsibility for that decision and for the consequences that result.

MOTIVES THAT CAN TRAP YOU

The term motive may be misleading since the term suggests a conscious decision, whereas motives are often not conscious. You can save yourself much grief by recognizing when you are about to act on the basis of the following common but erroneous motives.

Solving Problems for Others

Doing for others what they need to do for themselves encourages dependence and powerlessness. Attempting to solve problems for others that only they can solve for themselves (for example, making decisions) interferes with their ability to solve those problems.

Producing Adjustment

By the term adjustment I mean attempting to make other people contented (and preferably happy) with their situation in life, without helping them question whether they want to be happy with their situation, or whether they want a new situation. For example, a depressed person given medication to help him or her cope without being helped to consider alternatives and make decisions has not been helped much.

Helping others cope with a difficult situation is different from producing adjustment. People who function well in a situation will indeed be well-adjusted because they can cope with that situation while actively working to change their lot within the limits imposed by that situation.

The case of an adolescent I worked with is an example of what happens when well-intentioned people try to change others for the better. Jim had a domineering mother and a passive, occasionally violent father. He felt he couldn't rebel because his religion required him to honor and obey his parents and even to feel grateful to them. The more he tried to adjust himself to the situation, the more powerless and depressed he felt until he was finally hospitalized. He felt he should be able to cope and felt guilty that he couldn't. As long as his efforts (as well as those of others) were aimed at his making an adjustment to the situation, he continued to be severely depressed. He had learned to tell himself: "There's something wrong with me. I should be happy and content; I should be able to get along, I should be able to function as well as everyone else." Other teenagers were not as contented as he thought they were, but he didn't see this.

Jim learned to function within his difficult and frustrating situation only when he began to understand and accept the fact that he did not have to *like* the situation, that he did not have to pretend to himself that he liked the situation, that he did not have to keep telling himself that he should be happy in the situation.

If you know the story of Procrustes, you may remember that he was famous for "adjusting" his guests to the exact length of the bed in which they were to sleep by either stretching them out if they were too short or chopping them down a bit if they were too long. The desire to help others accept and be happy in a situation in which they are miserable may lead to a Procrustean effort that leaves them even more powerless.

Producing Conformity

We have expectations of how people should think, feel, and act. Our culture—especially the media, what we read, other people—continually reinforces these expectations. When we find someone with a problem, we spontaneously expect this person to think, feel, and act in certain ways; we expect others to conform to our ideas, and if they don't, we take notice. My child gets in trouble in school and I instinctively want him to conform enough to stay out of trouble. I may put aside these expectations long enough to listen and understand without imposing my own expectations and judgments; I want to tell him how he must behave instead of listening. An adolescent client tells me about her difficulty in getting along with her peers, and her mannerisms make it obvious to me why her peers reject her; I instinctively want her to conform to the minimal standards she needs for getting along with others, if for no other reason than for her own happiness. Yet if I try to get her to conform, I become either a rescuer or a persecuter. A student comes into my office, unhappy about a low grade that resulted from his not following directions, and I find myself wanting to blame him for not following directions. Acting on such impulses may easily focus only on helping others conform without enabling them to accept responsibility for their own behavior. Mere conformity does not produce genuinely cooperative, responsible individuals. People who merely conform do not act out of concern for others but to protect their own position within the group.

Molding and Shaping Others

Uncritical acceptance of our own impulses to influence others may lead us to discourage autonomy and independence in others. I remember two students saying that their reason for wanting to teach was the opportunity to mold students. In both instances I found their motives both ironic and potentially dangerous for the students they might have. One of these potential teachers was female, the other was male. The young woman wanted to teach young children because they were so easy to influence, but her own immature behavior left questions about her ability to encourage responsible behavior. The male, a man in his middle twenties, wanted to teach high school students, but he was so rigid in his thinking that his student-teaching supervisor, a faithful Baptist and hardly a radical was agitated and upset by the young man's reactionary attitudes regarding his authority as a teacher. I wouldn't want either of these people teaching my children because I would be afraid that they would learn only to obey, and not to think and act on their own.

"Doing Good"

Of all the motives for helping others, doing good may seem the most innocent. We hope that good comes of our efforts or we would not act in the first place. On the other hand, doing something in order to live up to an image of being good easily leads to helping others in ways they don't want and don't need.

Exercising Power

Helping others can become a way of exercising power over others rather than helping them. People who feel powerless may attempt to feel powerful by exercising power over others. This is very different from having a sense of power over one's own life. A sense of power over one's own life is essential in helping others. People with a sense of control over their own lives do not need power over others. Power over others is counter-productive since we can best increase our own power to think, feel, and act by helping others to increase their power over their own lives.

Every professional counselor, therapist, and psychiatrist knows of individuals who interfere in the lives of others in the guise of helping them, or who use others to satisfy their own wants. I feel suspicious of people whose primary impulse in helping is to solve problems for others, to produce adjustment or conformity, to mold others to their will or viewpoint or simply "to do good."

It would be easy to categorize and label people according to their motives. This would be easy, but labeling others makes it too easy to avoid examining our own motives. The problem is not some group of people "out there," but tendencies that exist in all of us. Each of us incorporates within ourselves all the contradictions of our culture and our society. Labeling individuals merely serves to attach blame to persons, rather than to examine patterns of behavior we are all capable of.

Effectiveness begins with awareness. When we recognize our own suspect motives, we can act to counter them, realizing that we are shaped by our culture, and that it would be surprising if we were not influenced by our culture. A simple example: If I ask my son to take out the garbage and he gives me a hard time, I want him to conform. If I then bend all my efforts into making him conform I may easily lose sight of what I am actually doing to him when I focus on making him into an obedient and respectful individual. By focusing all my efforts into making him conform, I deprive him of his autonomy, his power to act, to accept responsibility, to think, and feel, and create. Of course a single incident over a bag of garbage or even many bags of garbage will not produce such an effect. Yet teachers see many children each year who are able to conform but do not really know how to cooperate as responsible, independent, thinking individuals.

As my children grow, I look forward to being able to do more and more *with* them instead of *for* them. Yet at times, like every parent, I find myself pulling back, wanting them to wait until they're older, capable though they may be. I want to play it safe. The impulse is well-meaning, and well-intentioned, but do I want to protect them for their sake, or for mine? When we don't recognize the mixed nature of our own motives and impulses, we are likely to distort our own responsibilities. All relationships that involve helping are subject to the problem that our culture, our experience, the institutions we work for, and our own needs, all influence our motives. By treating our own motives with healthy suspicion, without blaming ourselves or feeling guilty, we can more easily act to prevent our motives from distorting our perceptions and our sense of responsibility.

SUMMARY

When a situation or a behavior does not have a direct and tangible effect on you, you can best help by not accepting responsibility for solving that problem, and instead devoting your energies to helping that person solve his or her own problem. The more helpless and incapable the other person seems, the more important it is to avoid making that person even more powerless by accepting responsibility for him or her. In the next chapter we will examine the responsibility of each person in a relationship.

chapter fifteen

Sorting out responsibility

No matter how much authority, power, or expertise you have, you are likely to find yourself feeling helpless and frustrated if you try to manipulate or control others' behavior. Power, expertise, or goodwill make little difference if you have to be responsible for everything. Treating others as if we should be able to change them results in conflict, discouragement, stress, anxiety, frustration, anger, and resentment. Acting on the assumption that others are responsible for their own behavior allows you to:

- Avoid being manipulated by others who attempt to make you responsible for their behavior.
- Encourage others to accept responsibility for their behavior.
- Focus on listening and problem solving instead of being drawn into cooperating with the other person's self-defeating behavior.

Basic Principle

Each person is responsible for his or her own behavior, including feelings, decisions, and actions.

Following this principle is essential to working effectively with others. The scope of an individual's power to make decisions and take action changes according to age, power, and other factors, but within these limits, each is responsible for his or her own feelings, decisions, and actions.

RESPONSIBILITY FOR FEELINGS AND ACTIONS

A key to being effective with people (and avoiding manipulation) is to realize that other people are responsible for their own feelings and that they, not you, have the power to change those feelings.

Our culture encourages us to believe that others are responsible for our feelings, good or bad ("you make me feel good," "she makes me feel bad," and so on). When people blame or credit others for their feelings, they deprive themselves of the power to change those feelings (Ellis 1971, 1977; Dreikurs 1953, 1967, 1971). Others are responsible for their own feelings; you can't accept responsibility for others' feelings without taking power away from them.

You can encourage others to accept their power to act by encouraging them to accept responsibility for their feelings.

Accepting responsibility does not mean accepting blame, nor does it mean accepting the situation without attempting to change it. Kay, a young woman, was upset about the way her boyfriend manipulated her feelings. He had a habit of baiting her to get her angry, and then of pointing out that, of course, she was responsible for her own feelings and had no call to blame him for those feelings. She felt stuck; she wanted to blame him but he had effectively defeated her attempts. On the other hand, she didn't want to blame herself. So she blamed herself and him.

Accepting responsibility for feelings means accepting that "I am responsible for my feelings and for what I do about them." I attempted to show Kay that:

- Other people do affect our feelings and it is absurd to deny it.
- Nevertheless, our feelings originate within us as a response to situations and we can choose other ways of responding.
- Accepting responsibility for our feelings gives us the freedom to find other ways to respond.

Where Kay was confused was in thinking that responding differently meant choosing to feel differently (a possibility). Choosing to respond differently could mean many things, of which feeling differently is only one. This is very different from a stoic acceptance of events over which one has no control. Accepting responsibility for feelings doesn't condemn the individual to bearing unacceptable situations; it frees him or her to make decisions about how better to cope with unacceptable situations. When Kay blamed either herself or her boyfriend, she remained powerless to do anything except what she was already doing. When she accepted responsibility for her feelings, she would be able to say to herself: "When my boyfriend tries to provoke me, I don't like this and I choose to feel upset. While it is understandable that I feel this way, my feelings are not helping me cope with this situation. What else can I do that would help me cope with the situation?" This same pattern of manipulation can occur in any relationship if you allow yourself to accept responsibility for the feelings of others.

RESPONSIBILITY FOR DECISIONS

Making decisions for others about what they should do makes them dependent on you and leaves you with a burden you don't need.

Making decisions for others makes you responsible for those decisions and also sets you up to be blamed if the person you are trying to help doesn't like the results.

By encouraging others to make their own decisions, you can do far more to help them gain a measure of control over their lives than you can by trying to make decisions for them. Some decisions can be right only in the sense that the person responsible for the decision makes it, that he or she accepts responsibility for it, and is willing to live with the consequences. For example, how do you ever know if you bought the right car or married the right person or went into the right occupation? A person who is encouraged to choose among alternatives learns to make decisions and to cope with the consequences of those decisions.

RESPONSIBILITY FOR BEHAVIOR

You can help others only in those areas in which they are willing to accept responsibility for their own behavior. You can encourage, urge, even coerce, but ultimately you cannot act for someone else. A philosopher once made the observation that "No one can die for you." This was parodied by another philosopher who remarked that "No one can take a bath for you." Of course both are true, and it is equally silly to accept responsibility for others in either matter.

The closer your relationship to the person you are working with, the easier it is to forget that you cannot act for that person. A parent who attempts to make a child's decisions for him deprives the child of the confidence and the experience of coping with problems. When situations arise in which the parents can no longer make decisions for their child, the child has no experience of making decisions; he is lost.

YOUR RESPONSIBILITY

Accepting responsibility for your decisions and actions allows you to avoid blaming others (or yourself) on the one hand, or making excuses for your behavior on the other hand. By admitting to yourself that you act because you have decided to, not because you think you should, you are free to change. If you erroneously tell yourself that you are doing something because you should or must or have to, you will easily fall into the trap of acting and feeling like a victim. By not accepting responsibility for your behavior, you may deprive yourself of the power you need to act effectively.

Consider the parent who does things for his child (from going to PTA meetings to sending the child to college), but who communicates to the child that these things are being done only because the parent feels he has a duty to do them. A certain friction, a certain resentment results in the relationship on both sides. Neither parent nor child feels good about either one giving or receiving help.

The same principle applies to your job. If you continually think of yourself as a victim who has no control over what happens to you, you will feel frustrated and resentful. One cause of job stress and the feeling of being burned out is the refusal to accept responsibility for choosing to act in a certain way. By saying "I have to" or "everyone expects me to," you can refuse to accept responsibility for your decisions. When we accept responsibility for choosing to act as we do, we are much less likely to feel victimized by others.

Responsibility for Feelings

Accepting responsibility for your own feelings allows you to avoid the trap of either rescuing or persecuting others because of your own feelings. It is also a key to using Strategy 4 (negotiating) effectively because it is by accepting your feelings as your own responsibility rather than blaming others that you are more likely to enlist the cooperation of others—even when they are the cause of your problem.

Basic Principle

> *Accept your feelings as your own without blaming or crediting others for those feelings.*

Consequences

> *You are less open to manipulation by others who attempt to manipulate you by making you feel guilty, angry, or upset.*

By accepting responsibility for your feelings, you are in a position to decide what to do about those feelings without spontaneously acting out your feelings.

No matter how helpless, dependent, or powerless other people may seem, they are capable of manipulating you if you credit or blame them for your feelings. (The next chapter describes such manipulation in detail.) The other person is influencing you as much as you are influencing him. People tend to make two mistakes in dealing with their own emotions, especially those involving anger and frustration. One mistake is trying to hide or deny the feelings. The other mistake in dealing with feelings is venting those feelings on others, possibly using the excuse of being "honest."

Attempting to hide or deny feelings seldom works, because those feelings influence our interactions. For example, suppose I am trying to help my daughter work on her math problems and I feel more and more frustrated and angry at what I see as her lack of cooperation. I can't successfully hide those feelings for long. I may pretend to be patient, but my true feelings are likely to reveal themselves in my tone of voice, my facial expression, my body posture. Particularly in a situation where you want others to be honest about their own feelings, you can encourage honesty by being honest about your own feelings without using image-centered language. Even when you choose not to express your feelings you need to be aware of them and to take them into account in making decisions about how to proceed. In the situation of helping my daughter with her math problems, I know that when I start to feel frustrated, we both need to take a break and come back when we feel more relaxed.

Shaming and blaming, inducing guilt feelings, name-calling, and criticizing are all ways of venting feelings on others. When someone isn't cooperating and you feel angry, it is very easy to say such things as "Why can't you cooperate?" (blaming) or "Can't you at least make an effort?" (shaming) or "Why do you ask for help if you don't want to cooperate?" Such sentences destroy the possibility of cooperation, at least for the moment.

The alternative to both these mistakes is to accept responsibility for your own feelings (thus avoiding the temptation to shame and blame others) and to express how you feel without dumping on the other person. When I can recognize my anger beginning to accumulate as I sense someone trying to manipulate me, and I can recognize what is happening and say to myself, "You are working yourself up; you are letting yourself be manipulated." If I say "I feel upset by what you are saying," I can express my anger without imposing that anger on the other person.

Accepting the idea that everyone (including you) is responsible for his or her own behavior allows you to avoid two traps: (1) mistaken interference in the problems of others resulting from a false sense of responsibility and (2) indifference resulting from not fully accepting responsibility for your own behavior.

Basic Principle

You are not and cannot be responsible for the behavior of others.

This is the opposite of what many people believe. Parents are told they are responsible for what their children do; teachers are told they are responsible for what their students do, and so on. Of course parents, teachers, counselors, and so on do have responsibility for what they do—how they exercise their responsibilities as parents, teachers, and counselors. However no one can control what others do. The more you try to do so, the more you focus on the other person's behavior instead of your own.

You are responsible for what you do to help, encourage, and influence others. You are responsible for what you do. While you are not responsible for the thoughts, feelings, and actions of others, you are responsible for what you do to influence others. If you give up on someone, if you act indifferently, you are responsible for these actions, and you have no reason to be surprised at the consequences that result.

The following anecdote illustrates both the dangers of taking on responsibility for the world and the rewards of accepting responsibility for one's own actions:

> I often feel I was born responsible. I have always taken on the worries of the world. During a very high-stress period in my life a few years ago, I was to the point that I would worry about what the news commentator was going to say about the economy. I literally became obsessed with the prime interest rate as it was climbing. My whole day was ruined if it went up at all—and a few years ago it climbed from 8% to 15% in a six-month time period. Our debt was staggering at that point—almost $950,000. I could hardly cope with car payments before I was married, than to handle interest of almost $250 a day and climbing.
> I had to learn to face the problem and not to ignore it. We had to set down strategies on how to physically handle that much debt. Thanks to the aid of Purdue's computers and some very good Prof. friends in the Ag. Econ. department we were able to restructure our debt and sell off unneeded assets. We survived! But I also survived mentally by learning that I couldn't be held responsible for the weather, the markets, or the economy. Worrying was a stifling, useless emotion that accomplished nothing but frustration and anger. I learned as a survival technique to be responsible for my own actions.*

SUMMARY

Feeling responsible easily leads to accepting responsibility for others instead of encouraging others to accept responsibility for themselves. Our culture encourages us to act in ways that seem responsible, but that work to rob others of their power to act by taking responsibility for them. Although we all influence one another, each of us is responsible for his or her own feelings and behavior. Helping others accept this responsibility is a step toward personal power.

---

*Comment supplied by a participant in a class on working effectively with people; used with permission.

chapter sixteen

The pattern of powerlessness and how to avoid it

Even after you understand the danger of assuming responsibility for solving other people's problems, it is still easy to accept too much responsibility and to keep others more dependent on you than they need to be. The result is often a pattern of mutual rescuing, persecuting, and feeling victimized. This pattern has been described by Stephen Karpman (1968), by Eric Berne (1964), and by Claude Steiner (1974).

RESCUING

Rescuing refers to attempts to help another person that aren't wanted or that reinforce irresponsible, dependent behavior. Typical examples of rescuing include:

- Continuing to take a child to school who habitually misses the bus.
- Giving advice on why smoking is bad for a friend's health and how it would be better if he or she would quit—and the friend hasn't asked for this advice.
- Continuing to lend someone money who makes little or no effort to return it.
- Continuing to reschedule someone for an appointment when he doesn't show up (and not charging for the time wasted).

PERSECUTING

Persecuting refers to using coercion or manipulation in an effort to help someone. Typical examples of persecuting behavior include:

- Nagging someone to go on a diet.
- Threatening someone with dire consequences to his or her health if he or she doesn't give up smoking.
- Threatening others in an attempt to change them.
- Interrogating.

In practice rescuing and persecuting are sometimes indistinguishable, as rescuing is itself often a subtle form of coercion.

FEELING VICTIMIZED

Feeling victimized refers to thinking and feeling as though one were powerless. Typical examples of feeling victimized include:

- Feeling frustrated and discouraged.
- Feeling resentful.
- Feeling ignored.
- Feeling unappreciated.
- Thinking that others should appreciate you more.
- Thinking that others should treat you better.

THE PATTERN OF RESCUING, PERSECUTING, FEELING VICTIMIZED

Basic Principle

In a cycle of rescuing, persecuting, and feeling victimized, both helper and person being helped will typically engage in rescuing, persecuting, and feeling victimized.

Being able to recognize when you are in such a cycle is the first step in extricating yourself. Once you see what is happening (or has already happened) you can use your skills to set limits, to renegotiate what you are willing to do, or to cope with attacks. First, however, you must recognize the pattern. We will examine nine typical steps in a cycle of rescuing, persecuting, and feeling victimized.

The following protocol describes what happens when one person attempts to help another without an adequate understanding of who has the problem and who has responsibility for the problem. Two people, designated *A* and *B*, are the protagonists. Note that both *A* and *B* engage in rescuing, persecuting, and feeling victimized.

1. *A* attempts to rescue *B*.
   "Let me show you how to solve this!"
2. *B* does not cooperate or is not properly appreciative.
   "I would rather do it myself."
3. *A* feels victimized because he is not succeeding.
   "Look how hard I try and *B* doesn't cooperate."
4. *A* persecutes *B* in an attempt to make *B* cooperate.
   "You are making a big mistake!"
5. *B* feels victimized.
   "Look how hard I try and no one appreciates my efforts!"
6. *B* persecutes *A* to get even.
   "I'm leaving until you get more sense!"
7. *A* feels victimized.
   "I feel so bad when this happens."
8. *B* relents and rescues *A* by reassuring *A*.
   "It's O.K."
9. *A* attempts to rescue *B* (back to step 1.)

"Let me help you...." These nine steps describe what tends to happen in a cycle of rescuing, persecuting, and feeling victimized. Knowing this pattern is useful in avoiding it. Knowing the pattern is also useful in recognizing and escaping when you have become trapped without realizing it. The four examples that follow illustrate how the pattern works itself out in common situations.

EXAMPLE 1:
A VALUES CONFLICT*

Attempting to help another person do "the right thing" can cause problems. In the following example a mother is upset because her teenage daughter has begun to smoke. The steps taken by the mother to get her daughter to change

*Example supplied by a teacher; used with permission.

quickly lead to a power struggle:

1. *A* attempts to rescue *B*

   "Why have you started to smoke? You know how bad it is for you!" [Mother takes problem as hers, even though it has no direct effect on her and even though she cannot control what her daughter does outside the house.]

2. *B* does not cooperate.

   Jackie keeps right on smoking, although not in front of her mother or father. [Jackie already feels defensive about her smoking and does not appreciate the efforts made by her mother.]

3. *A* feels victimized because she is not succeeding.

   Mother reports her feelings in this situation as follows. "I felt I had not been a good mother; I could not convince her to stop smoking, so I was a failure." [Note that mother feels victimized not because of what has happened, but because she feels *she* is responsible.]

4. *A* persecutes *B* in an attempt to make *B* cooperate.

   Mother threatens Jackie in an attempt to coerce her into stopping: "Jackie, if you don't stop smoking, I'm going to tell your grandparents." [Jackie has always wanted her grandparents' approval. When mother can't succeed by what she considers positive methods (i.e., rescuing) she turns to coercion.]

5. *B* feels victimized.

   Jackie feels backed into a corner. She doesn't want to give in and lose the battle; at the same time she hates the thought of her grandparents' disapproval.

6. *B* persecutes *A* to get back.

   Jackie stops speaking to her mother for the next several days and when she does speak, she is rude.

7. *A* feels victimized.

   Mother's reaction: "I was wondering what I had done to deserve this!" [Mother's reaction is typical; she doesn't see how her rescuing and persecuting creates the situation.]

8. *B* relents and rescues *A*.

   Jackie begins talking to her mother again when the situation cools off, but without the situation's being solved.

9. *A* attempts to rescue *B* [game starts over].

   Mother reports: "Several weeks later (after things had returned to normal) I tried again (with similar results)."

Mother reports, by the way, that after a year of smoking, her daughter decided *on her own* to stop smoking. By assuming that she was responsible for Jackie's behavior, Jackie's mother set herself up to rescue and persecute, and then, when these failed, to feel victimized.

Jackie's mother assumed she understood the problem without bothering to listen and reflect. Several years later, she found out what was behind the smoking:

> I found out later that Jackie had started to smoke because she had heard it would help you lose weight.

EXAMPLE 2:
COOPERATION BETWEEN EQUALS—
THE FISHERMEN*

Cooperation between equals is often tricky. Efforts to help may be subtle attempts to establish a position of superiority. The following situation is an excellent example of the jockeying for position and status that often underlies offers of help. This situation, precisely because of its triviality, demonstrates the real nature of rescuing and persecuting as means of achieving a subtle superiority over others.

Situation: Two men are out on a lake, fishing from a small boat.

1. A attempts to rescue B.
   "Gee, John, we've been fishing since six this morning and you haven't caught a thing. Want to try one of my minnows when you finish your lunch? I've caught six good fish over by that log." [A's offer is genuine, but is also a subtle putdown of John.]
2. B is not appreciative.
   "No, I'll keep using these night crawlers."
3. A feels victimized and persecutes B in an attempt to make B cooperate.
   "This time of year on this lake night crawlers are no good. You can fish all day and never get a bite. I don't know why you're so stubborn."
4. B feels victimized and persecutes A to even the score.
   "You keep giving advice like that and you'll be swimming back to shore. Besides, you didn't do so hot over on Swede Lake last week, remember?" [B retaliates; the argument is now definitely not about worms but about who is the superior fisherman.]
5. A feels victimized.
   [Silence from the back of the boat for five minutes.] A is thinking, "I try to be helpful and look what happens." He doesn't realize how his initial behavior created the situation.

*Example supplied by a graduate student; used with permission.

8. *B* relents, rescuing *A* with reassurance.
"Of course, Swede Lake is a tough lake this time of year." [*B* is concerned that he has gone too far.]
9. *A* attempts to rescue *B* (back to the top and start over.)
"Want a minnow, John?" [*A* takes *B*'s reassurance as an invitation to repeat his original offer.]

The fact that neither fisherman sees the pattern in which he participates keeps the game going. John sees his behavior as quite innocent and well intentioned. John's friend, on the other hand, understands very well that to accept the kind of help he is offered is to accept a putdown, however mild (thus explaining his willingness to throw John out of the boat). The man who described this incident pointed out that "I have been in both ends of the boat in the past and have played both parts at different times."

It is not the offer of a minnow that creates the problem, but the manner in which the offer was made. Attempts to rescue others communicates the message: "I am superior, so I will help you." This message creates resistance and resentment in the other person. The "innocent" rescuer can't understand why his offers of assistance are refused. The payoff for rescuing others is often a feeling of superiority. Unfortunately for the rescuer however, the price extracted is often a feeling of frustration and powerlessness when help is taken for granted, rejected, or resented.

EXAMPLE 3:
SUPPLYING UNWANTED EXPERTISE*

Rescuing often begins when one person sees another having difficulty and offers to supply the missing expertise. The following dialogue takes place in a classroom, but the same dialogue might have taken place anywhere.

Situation: A teacher offers help to a student.

1. *A* attempts to rescue *B*.
"I see you are having a little difficulty. Would you like for me to show you how to do it?" [This question would not necessarily lead to a rescue; it is a rescue statement only in the light of what follows.]
2. *B* does not cooperate and is not appreciative.
"No, I want to do it myself." [Note that this is a perfectly reason-

*Example supplied by a teacher; used with permission.

able statement, and if *A* had withdrawn at this point, no rescue would have taken place.]

3. *A* feels victimized.

   A thinks: "I just wanted to help the student." [Note that *A* feels victimized not because of what happens, but because of what she tells herself when her offer is declined.]

4. *A* persecutes *B*

   "The class is getting restless while you take your time. Let me show you how to do it." [When *B* does not accept the offer of help, *A* attempts to impose the help.]

5. *B* feels victimized.

   The student feels trapped. The teacher won't leave him alone, and he feels angry and resentful.

6. *B* persecutes *A*.

   The student says, "Here, you do it!" and walks away. [The student cannot openly defy the teacher, so he defeats the teacher by appearing to give in, but without cooperating.]

7. *A* feels victimized.

   The teacher realizes she is trapped. Realizing her mistake, she extricates herself from the power struggle by walking over to the student and apologizing: "I'm sorry I didn't let you finish your project. Come on back."

8. *B* relents and rescues *A*.

   "I'm sorry Mrs. *A*. I know you were trying to help me. Would you help me?"

9. *A* attempts to rescue *B* (back to the top).

   In this situation the pattern ended with Step 8.

Such patterns as the one above may end temporarily only to be continued on another day. The teacher who described this situation writes:

> After becoming aware of this rescue game, I'm sure I couldn't count the number of times I've used it with my students, all the time thinking that I was just trying to help. I can see what a circle it is now.
> It is hard to let others do some things which we could do better and faster for them.

The teacher could have avoided a power struggle by tactfully withdrawing when the student expressed a wish to work on his task by himself. By assuming that the student's slowness was her responsibility, she created a problem and was then surprised at what happened. In a situation where you want to help, that help needs to be given in a way that allows the other person to retain control over the situation.

EXAMPLE 4:
BEING TRAPPED INTO RESCUING

Rescues are not always initiated by a rescuer. In some situations you may be manipulated into rescuing. The following example shows what can happen when *B* invites a rescue.

Situation: Mrs. B wants help from *A* for her son Jason.

1. *B* invites *A* to rescue her.
    "You've got to help me. I can't do a thing with Jason [her son] here...." [Proceeds to give a long history of Jason's misbehavior.]
2. *A* attempts to rescue *B*.
    "Well, I can give you some things to do that will help you cope better with Jason. When we can get parents to change the way they handle situations the children often change." [*A* proceeds to outline a program of changes that Mrs. *B* can make.]
3. *B* does not cooperate and is not appreciative.
    "Yes, but I've tried everything. I want you to do something with Jason so he'll behave." [Mrs. *B* feels defensive about her ability as a parent and feels that she is being told that Jason's behavior is her fault. She wants *A* to change Jason.]
4. *A* feels victimized.
    A feels that he was hired to help, is doing his best, but is being dumped on by Mrs. *B*. He doesn't realize that she has set him up so that she can defeat him by proving that he can't do anything to help Jason either—thus vindicating her behavior as his mother.
5. *A* persecutes *B*.
    "I can't help you if you're not willing to try." [*A* has been caught in the trap. By persecuting Mrs. *B*, he only confirms her beliefs that he can't or won't help her.]
6. *B* feels victimized.
    Mrs. *B* feels victimized, reinforcing her belief that she is well intentioned and wants help, but that the experts just blame her instead of helping her.
7. *B* persecutes *A*.
    "No one can handle Jason; he's always been this way. We've never been able to do a thing with him." [Mrs. *B* defeats *A*'s efforts to help

her by repeating her inability and unwillingness to change, and implying that *A* should do something.]
8. *A* feels victimized.

    The more Mrs. *B* resists his attempts to help, the more he feels victimized and defeated. If *A* recognized what was happening, he could stop the game by refusing to get upset and by not making further suggestions until they are asked for.
9. *B* relents and rescues *A* by reassuring him.

    "I don't mean to get on you. I'm sure you have a lot of education and everything. I just want you to help Jason behave better. [Mrs. *B* backs off to avoid a confrontation. Clients sometimes attempt to back off when they realize that the person working with them is becoming upset. Clients tend to perceive professionals as people of high status and authority and are reluctant to push them too far.]
10. *A* attempts to rescue *B* (back to step 1).

    A feels that *B* may have a change of heart and begins again to discuss what she might do about Jason....

Being rescued brings attention and special service from others without the effort of helping oneself. Successful rescuees often are adept at getting others to do their work or to make exceptions on their behalf. A really successful rescuee is a super manipulator. Unfortunately, rescuees often feel powerless, even though they manipulate others successfully. Deeply discouraged about their ability to solve their problems, they become trapped by their own success in manipulating others.

AVOIDING THE TRAPS

The following guidelines are useful in avoiding the trap of rescuing, persecuting, and feeling victimized:

- Decide who has the problem.
- Be aware of your own attitudes and feelings.
- Get a commitment of cooperation from the other person.
- Avoid commitments you are unwilling to make.
- Treat the other person as an equal.
- Don't pretend to know more than you do.
- Encourage a sense of control.

Decide who has the problem. Rescuing behavior is often the result of accepting problems of others as one's own. As soon as you take on responsibility for solving another's problem, you are steering toward a rescue relationship.

Be aware of your own attitudes and feelings. Awareness of your own attitudes and feelings is often a good source of information of what is going on in a relationship. For example, when you notice you are beginning to feel angry or frustrated in working with someone, it is usually a good sign that you are about to become involved in (or are already in) a rescue relationship.

Get a commitment of cooperation from the other person. Cooperation from the person you want to help is essential. If the other person makes no commitment to cooperate, go no further, or you may quickly find yourself in a rescue relationship. You can be of use only in those areas where the other person is willing to hire you. Situations in which you supply all the effort quickly leads both to rescuing and persecuting.

In our eagerness to help we may easily fall into the trap of not waiting for the other person to make an effort on his or her behalf. Your emotional response is often a good indication of whether you are doing more than your share. When you feel you are doing all the work and the other person is doing nothing, you may be rescuing. Doing more than your share not only doesn't help you or the other person, it is likely to lead to discouragement, frustration, and persecution. At some point a person who wants help needs to make an effort to help himself. You can use Strategy 4 (negotiating with others) when necessary to clarify what you are going to do and what the other person is going to do.

Avoid commitments you are unwilling to make. Helping someone only because you think you should quickly leads to rescuing and persecuting, and then to feeling victimized when your efforts are not appreciated. If you do things you feel unwilling to do, you will feel resentful. This resentment will come out in one way or another and will result in resentment from the person you are trying to help.

The question arises, "But don't we all have to do things we don't like? You can't just do what you like." Being *willing* to do something and *liking* to do something are not the same thing. I work on my income taxes because I want to get them done, not because I like doing them. What we are willing to do is revealed by our actions, not by what we say or by what we tell ourselves.

Telling ourselves that we are only doing something because we should is a way of not admitting that we have decided to do that thing, no matter how much we may like or dislike it.

Don't agree to do something that you feel unwilling to do. Setting limits to the help you give will not destroy your relationships with others and may very well improve them. When you set limits on the help you give, both you and others will know that when you agree to help, you do so willingly. Once again, Strategy 4 (negotiating) is an excellent means for setting limits.

Treat the other person as an equal. If you feel or act superior, this encourages the other person to feel inferior, resentful, and uncooperative.

People who want to be rescued may encourage you to feel superior in order to get you to take care of their needs. Beware when someone says to you, "You understand this and I don't. Show me how to do it (i.e., do it *for* me)." Other people may use this strategy to make you feel good about rescuing, but once involved in a rescue pattern, you may eventually suffer the consequences of becoming involved in the rescue game.

Don't pretend to know more than you do. You don't have to answer every question or solve every problem. Even if someone asks you for a solution, keep in mind that providing a solution may involve you in a rescue. Other people may expect you to be a magician, and you may even be able to convince them that you are a magician—part of the time. However attempting to live up to expectations to be a magician eventually ends in your feeling victimized when you don't succeed. Also, when you don't succeed, people who have treated you as a magician will persecute you.

Encourage a sense of control. People who have difficulty coping with problems often have little sense of being able to control what happens to them (Freire 1970). Encouraging a sense of control encourages responsible action. When people feel that their actions have consequences, they are much more likely to accept responsibility.

A Caution About Helping Others in Rescue Patterns

When you find others—especially friends, family members, or people with whom you work every day—who are in a rescue pattern, proceed with caution. As a rule, the best way to proceed is to stay out. Strategy 1 (listening) is often a good way to avoid taking sides.

It is easy to become involved in rescuing others from rescue relationships. Attempts on your part to change them are likely to involve you in a rescue pattern. People who feel that part of their role as parents, bosses, administrators, teachers, and so on, is to rescue and persecute others will resist giving up the behavior—after all their self-image is tied up in this behavior, and change is likely to be threatening.

SUMMARY

Working with others ends in mutual frustration and discouragement when both sides become enmeshed in a pattern of rescuing, persecuting, and feeling victimized. It is difficult not to accept responsibility for the problems of others, especially when those problems desperately need solutions. It is easy to make the irrational assumption that, because we want desperately to help and because a solution is desperately needed, we can find a solution by accepting responsibility for the problem and by having good intentions. It is easy to irrationally believe that if we only care desperately enough, a solution can and will be found and that we can create a happy ending if we only want it badly enough. Unfortunately feelings of desperation result in poor judgment more often than in solutions and happy endings.

Working with other people sometimes ends in a "rescue game," because helping is often extolled as virtuous and good in itself, whether or not the person being helped is encouraged to be more independent and responsible or more dependent and powerless. Our culture encourages us to think that taking on the problems of others is generous, selfless, and even noble. The heavy cost we may pay is seen not as an indication that something is wrong but as proof of the nobility of helping (Steiner, 1974).

You are more likely to succeed in getting others to accept responsibility and solve problems when they feel they have power over what they do and over what happens to them. Effectiveness consists not of solving problems for others, but of encouraging them to take back the power they have given away.

chapter seventeen

Guidelines for using what you've learned

The guidelines that follow apply to all the skills and strategies. If they could be summed up in one sentence, it might be this: You can learn the skills and strategies only by using them.

Practice with neutral situations in which you have a high probability of success. You are not likely to be effective in using a skill until it becomes a relatively automatic part of your behavior. We tend to use a new idea or technique to deal with our biggest problem. When the technique fails to get results we become discouraged and give up. Try the skills and strategies first in:

- Neutral or low-threat situations.
- Highly structured situations.
- Situations with little danger of serious consequences.

As you build up skill you will become more confident in using the techniques. Also, you are more likely to be successful in difficult situations because you will have more skill.

The more formal and structured your relationship with the other person, the easier you will find it to use the techniques successfully. For example, your relationship with a boss or with clients is relatively well defined. You will find it much easier to use the techniques with them than with members of your family.

The techniques will work in close personal relationships, but it is more difficult to use them consistently and effectively. When I am with a client, I orient myself in a certain way: I am there to listen, to help the other person think through problems, to help where I can. When I get home, my own interests come into play much more; I am not oriented to do a certain job. As a result I may find it much more difficult to listen to my own child than to a child who comes in to see me in a clinical setting.

In addition, close personal relationships often are built on long-established patterns. New behavior is more noticeable and is likely to be questioned. Do use the skills in your personal relationships—that is where you will find they have the biggest reward; don't be discouraged to find that you can apply the skills much more easily in more defined situations at first.

Make your nonverbal behavior congruent with what you say. A person who smiles and says, "I'm glad to see you," in a strong, enthusiastic tone of voice is more convincing than someone who says the same words without expression. Tone of voice, facial expression, physical proximity, and body gestures communicate messages about attitudes and feelings. When these messages complement and reinforce one another they are said to be *congruent*. When different messages appear to contradict one another the other person is likely to feel confused and distrustful. The more congruent you are in your everyday conversation, the more congruent you are likely to be in using new techniques. On the other hand, using the skills can help increase congruence.

Pay attention to your tone of voice. Tone of voice is one of the things most likely to sabotage your efforts. If your tone of voice communicates blame, guilt, inattention, condescension, or other image-centered messages, your words may not be believable. The voice tones which most often sabotage an otherwise sincere message are sounding judgmental, sounding whiny (complaining), and sounding dead. A judgmental, critical tone of voice communicates a sense of trying to control, of wanting power over others rather than a desire to share your power with others. Others will react defensively and with suspicion. A whining, complaining tone of voice communicates a sense of powerlessness, which leads others to wonder how you can help them when you yourself seem so powerless. A dead, expressionless tone of voice communicates a sense of boredom and lack of involvement.

Use the other person's language. The essence of establishing rapport with others is being able to enter into the other person's point of view without losing or surrendering your own separateness and individuality. Effective communication requires that you share, at least for the moment, the reality of the person you are talking with. On the other hand, attempts to imitate another's behavior in order to establish rapport can be overdone. Working with adolescents illustrates this: If you use language, gestures, and tone of voice characteristic of parents and teachers, adolescents won't listen to you—you are immediately identified as one of the enemy. On the other hand, if you try to talk with them as though you were one of them, they will be equally put off.

In particular, pay attention to the words the other person uses that indicate whether he or she is thinking primarily in visual, auditory, or kinesthetic (feelings and physical movement) terms. It can be important to use the mode used by the other person. If he is using primarily words that suggest *seeing* and you use words that refer to *feeling*, you may lose the other person. I remember teaching a class on communication techniques for teachers. At the end of each class I would ask how people *felt* about what had happened during that class. One evening when I did this, a woman in the class finally overcame her reluctance to express her frustration and asked, "Why do you always ask us how we *feel* about the class? I never know what to say." When she said this, I asked her, "How did the class *look* to you tonight?" She smiled and gave a positive reply.

Be aware of the limits of a relationship based on power. You will be most effective (and you will find yourself most satisfied) by establishing a pattern of cooperation based on mutual power. Cooperation based on mutual power allows each person to exercise responsibility over his or her own behavior and relieves each of the burden of responsibility for coercing or enticing others. Unfortunately there are situations in which such cooperation is severely limited because one person insists on using power.

A relationship based mainly on power is very different (and much less satisfying) than a relationship based on cooperation. In such a relationship openness may be mistaken for weakness. For example, diplomats may not reveal their true thoughts or feelings when dealing with other diplomats because they might reveal something that could be used against them or their country. In such situations the ability to do this is a strength.

The skills and strategies will help you to survive in such situations, because when properly used they allow you to enter into the other person's world and thus understand and avoid unnecessary conflicts. The skills and strategies will also allow you to operate from a position that gives you power over your own behavior—something that others can not take away from you unless you let them. This is a great advantage in working with people who have power over you or who are extremely manipulative. For example, if, in your boss's world, people do not reveal their feelings, then you may not want to reveal your own feelings—unless you choose to do so in order to create a confrontation. You can use the power you have over your own behavior to mask your feelings, when appropriate, in a congruent way.

Unfortunately, in order to survive in a relationship, many of us learn to hide our feelings and true thoughts in situations in which there is no need to do so. What we have used to survive easily becomes the standard for all our relationships, and we are left poorer and less effective and less happy than we might be.

Observe and experiment. You learn the techniques by trying them and observing what happens. Experiment with different wording. By experimenting you will find that differences in wording do make a difference.

Observing the other person is an important part of any communication process. You learn what is effective by being aware of how the other person responds. It is possible for you to see and hear far more than you now do. In learning any skill, as you become more skillful you begin to notice more and more details that you were formerly oblivious of. When a carpenter walks through a house, he notices details that noncarpenters don't even imagine. When a plant pathologist walks through a field, she notices things that even the farmer misses. By learning communication skills you can learn to be aware of nuances of language and gesture that you hadn't dreamed existed. (For specific exercises concerned with becoming a better observer, I suggest *The Structure of Magic I and II* by Bandler and Grinder.)

Begin by using a formula. By learning a formula first, you will have a base from which to depart. Unless you can use the formula you have only a vague, general idea of the particular skill you want to use.

Prepare your initial response in advance. In situations in which you are approaching another person, know what you are going to say in advance. If necessary, write out your position and your basic statements so that you will know you are well prepared.

Once in a situation, don't think about your own position or what you will say. That's why you have prepared in advance (when possible)—so that you don't have to think about your own position and can pay attention to the other person.

A big danger in teaching techniques to people is that they assume they can use the technique to bring about a desired result, much like turning on a switch to light a dark room. They say the magic words and are surprised when they don't see any results. The skills will help you communicate more effectively, but they do nothing by themselves.

Again, practice, preferably in neutral situations. You are not likely to be effective in using a skill until the skill becomes a relatively automatic part of your behavior.

Avoid a cookbook approach. While using a formula is useful in learning the skills, there is no formula for handling a particular situation. The intent of this book is not to tell you what to do or to tell you what is right, but to increase your alternatives. If you have three or four or five ways of responding to a situation, you have more freedom and flexibility than if you have only one or two ways of responding to that situation.

Occasionally record your conversations. An excellent strategy for learning to hear what you say and how you sound is to tape record yourself in a problem situation. We are often unaware of what we say (we only think we know) and of how we sound. Here is an exercise I have used with classes and workshops that many people have found helpful:

- Record yourself in a conversation, preferably a problem-solving situation. The conversation should preferably go on for more than five minutes so that the other person will get used to the tape recorder.
- Put the tape away for several weeks. You want to be able to listen to the tape as if it were made by another person. After several weeks you will be able to analyze the tape more objectively.
- Transcribe two minutes of the tape that seem characteristic of the conversation. Note the exact words, the pauses, the tone of voice used. This is work—you will have to listen to a particular passage many times to get the exact wording, but the very process of listening many times to the same passage will usually reveal many nuances you didn't notice at first.
- Analyze the transcript, answering these questions:
    Who did most of the talking?
    Who has the problem?
    Are there image-centered questions or statements and how could they be changed or deflected?
    What does your tone of voice communicate?

Request specific feedback when criticized. When someone calls a behavior of yours to your attention, ask that person to be specific. You can use the techniques listed under "changing image-centered criticism to problem-centered criticism. The more you find out about your own spontaneous and unintended behavior, the better idea you will have about how your behavior affects the responses of others.

Evaluate your behavior, not yourself. We tend to judge ourselves because we have been taught that it is virtuous to judge oneself and feel guilty—and that it is bad to refuse to judge oneself.

When we are concerned with judging ourselves we tend to act ineffectively; when we judge our behavior without judging ourselves, we are more likely to change.

Pay attention to the situation. You will act more effectively when you consider your immediate situation before deciding whether to use a particular technique. Probably the most common of all misapplications of techniques is to think you recognize a situation you have seen before, and then to try what worked in the past. Effective behavior is based on being aware of what is happening now, not by applying what worked in the past.

We tend to act ineffectively not because we don't know what to do, but because we aren't aware of what is happening in the immediate situation. In teaching techniques, I am asked the "right way" to handle a particular type of situation. Fortunately or unfortunately, there is no one right way you can prepare in advance that is certain to work. For example, teachers have often been exhorted to praise their students. But students (and others) often react negatively to praise. This is an important point, because as human beings we sometimes want to have rules that guarantee success. However it is only by being aware of what is happening on a moment-to-moment basis that we have the information we need to respond effectively.

When we feel concerned about how we are doing, we tend to act less effectively. In general, most of us have been taught to be concerned about how *we* are doing. The more sensitive or public the situation, the more we tend to feel concerned about how we are doing.

Focus on long-term change. We tend to see what we do as effective when we see an immediate change in behavior—even if this short-run change is part of a large pattern of negative cooperation. For example:

- A parent nags her child to do homework, and finally the child does the homework, but nagging must be repeated the next night. When parent does not remind and nag, the child doesn't do the homework.
- An employment counselor badgers and cajoles a client into going for a particular job interview—the client eventually goes, but is late or for

some other reason doesn't make the right impression and doesn't get the job.
- A physician threatens a patient with dire consequences if he does not quit smoking; the patient agrees to quit, and even succeeds for a short time, but then starts again.

What seems to be effective may be part of a larger pattern that encourages powerlessness and irresponsibility in the other person.

Be aware of your own preconceived ideas and adjust your behavior to compensate. We tend to act more effectively when we do not form a preconceived idea of what should happen. The trick is to catch yourself making up your mind *before* you have all the facts and *before* you hear what the other person has to say. Strategy 1 (listening) is almost always an effective way to counteract this tendency. Especially in situations in which you want to get others to take responsibility (Strategy 3) or in which you want to negotiate because you have a problem with another's behavior, use Strategy 1 and listen and then move on to the other strategy.

Don't use the skills to try to manipulate others. Using techniques to manipulate others tends to be ineffective in the long run. Learning a technique as a means of manipulating others does not encourage open communication over an extended period of time.

Challenge your own and others' ideas about what you "should" do. When we do what we think is expected of us, we tend to see our behavior as effective. For example, it is very easy for me as a parent to offer advice without ever noticing whether or not my advice is being listened to. I find it easy to assume that I am effective because I am doing what "good parents" are expected to do.

It is very difficult to lay aside our existing ideas about effective behavior and actually look at what is happening and ask:

- What is going on here and now?
- What effect am I having?
- What are the probable effects of my behavior?
- Am I helping?

What we think is the right thing to do, what others expect of us, or even what this book suggests, is not necessarily what a particular situation calls for. Because there can be no formula for what to do in a given situation, people who always do what is expected of them end up acting inappropriately much of the time. The image we have of ourselves as the good employee, parent, teacher, nurse, spouse, administrator, and so on, makes it difficult for us to recognize when we are not effective. The more rigid and detailed our image, the more difficulty we will have in recognizing our own ineffectiveness.

Let your mind handle the work of choosing and using the skills. Consciously prepare (if possible) beforehand. Consciously analyze what happened afterward. But in the situation itself, give your full attention to the other person and let yourself respond without consciously thinking about the skills. Your mind is quite capable of using the skills without your having to consciously attend to what you are doing. Attending to what you are doing instead of to the other person takes your mind off the task at hand. In driving a car, if you put all your attention on the mechanics of driving, you can't watch the road. Similarly, if you put all your attention on what you are going to do, you can't pay attention to what's going on.

SUMMARY

Awareness of the problems in learning and using techniques is useful in avoiding discouragement and giving up. In particular, attempting to use a technique in a difficult situation before you have acquired skill is likely to result in failure. Attempting to use a technique first with people who know you well is also likely to result in failure. People who know us well often have a vested interest in keeping our behavior predictable, and so they are likely to discourage new behavior.

Techniques are tools; they will not work by themselves. You must find the conditions under which they will function. Perhaps the most important factor in using a technique is matching your tone of voice, facial expression, and gestures to the message you wish to communicate. Saying the words is not enough: communication requires matching verbal and nonverbal messages for it to be believable.

The techniques in this book are not ways of changing others, but ways of changing your own behavior. When you change your behavior—what you say, how you feel, what you think—others, in order to respond to your new behavior, will change.

References

Alberti, R.E. and Emmons, M.L. *Your perfect right*. San Luis Obispo, California: Impact Publishers, 1978.
Bandler, R. and Grinder, J. *The structure of magic I*. Palo Alto, California: Science and Behavior Books, Inc., 1975.
Bandler, R. and Grinder, J. *The structure of magic II*. Palo Alto, California: Science and Behavior Books, Inc., 1976.
Bassin, A., Brattler, T.E. and Rackin, R.L. (Eds.) *The reality therapy reader*. New York: Harper and Row, Publishers, 1976.
Berne, E. *Games people play*. New York: Grove Press, 1964.
Berne, E. *Beyond games and scripts*. New York: Grove Press, Inc., 1976.
Bolton, R. *People skills*. Englewood Cliffs, New Jersey: Prentice-Hall, Inc., 1979.
Brammer, L.M. *The helping relationship: Process and skills*. Englewood Cliffs, New Jersey: Prentice-Hall, Inc., 1979.
Carkhuff, R.R. *The art of helping III*. Amherst, Massachusetts: Human Resource Development Press, 1977.
Carkhuff, R.R. *The art of helping IV*. Amherst, Massachusetts: Human Resource Development Press, 1980.
Carkhuff, R.R. and Anthony, W.A. *The skills of helping*. Amherst, Massachusetts: Human Resource Development Press, 1979.

Cotler, S.B. and Guerra, J.J. *Assertion training.* Champaign, Illinois: Research Press Company, 1976.

Dinkmeyer, D. and Dreikurs, R. *Encouraging children to learn: The encouragement process.* Englewood Cliffs, New Jersey: Prentice-Hall, Inc., 1963.

Dreikurs, R. *Fundamentals of Adlerian psychology.* Chicago: Alfred Adler Institute of Chicago, 1953.

Dreikurs, R. *The challenge of parenthood* (Rev. ed). New York: Hawthorn Books, 1958.

Dreikurs, R. *Psychodynamics, psychotherapy, and counseling: Collected papers of Rudolf Dreikurs, M.D.* Chicago: Alfred Adler Institute of Chicago, 1967.

Dreikurs, R. *Social Equality: The challenge of today.* Chicago: Henry Regnery, 1971.

Dreikurs, R., Grunwald, B., and Pepper, F. *Maintaining sanity in the classroom.* New York: Harper and Row, Publishers, 1971.

Ellis, A. *Growth through reason: Verbatim cases in rational-emotive therapy.* North Hollywood, California: Wilshire Book Company, 1971.

Ellis, A. *Reason and emotion in psychotherapy.* Secaucus, N.J.: The Citadel Press, 1977.

Ellis, A. *How to raise an emotionally healthy, happy child.* Hollywood, Cal.: Wilshire, 1978.

Ellis, A., and Harper, R.A. *A new guide to rational living.* California: Wilshire Book Company, 1975.

Egan, G. *Interpersonal living.* Monterey, California: Brooks Cole Publishing Company, 1976.

Egan, G. *The skilled helper: A model for systematic helping and interpersonal relating.* Monterey, California: Brooks Cole Publishing Company, 1975.

Freire, P. *Pedagogy of the oppressed.* (Trans. M.B. Ramos) New York: Herder and Herder, 1970.

Gazda, G.M. (Ed.) *Basic approaches to group psychotherapy and group counseling.* Springfield, Illinois: Charles C. Thomas, 1975.

Gazda, G.M. *Human relations development.* Boston: Allyn and Bacon, Inc., 1973.

Glasser, W. *Reality therapy.* New York: Harper and Row, Pub., 1965.

Glasser, W. *Schools without failure.* New York: Harper and Row, Publishers, 1969.

Gordon, T. *T.E.T.:* Teacher effectiveness training. New York: D. McKay, 1974.

Hall, E.T. *The silent language.* Garden City, New York: Doubleday, 1959.

Hackney, H. and Nye, S. *Counseling strategies and objectives.* Englewood Cliffs, New Jersey: Prentice-Hall, Inc., 1979.

Ivey, A.E. and Authier, J. *Microcounseling: Innovations in interviewing, counseling, psychotherapy, and psychoeducation.* (Second Ed.) Springfield, Illinois: Charles C. Thomas, 1978.

Jakubowski, P. and Lange, A.J. *The assertive option.* Champaign, Illinois: Research Press Company, 1978.

Karpman, Stephen B. Script drama analysis. *Transactional Analysis Bulletin* 1968, 7, 26, 39-43.

Knapp, M.L. *Essentials of nonverbal communication.* New York: Holt, Rinehart and Winston, 1980.

Korzybski, A. *Science and sanity.* Lancaster, Pennsylvania: Lancaster Press, 1933.

Lange, A.J. and Jakubowski, P. *Responsible assertive behavior.* Champaign, Illinois: Research Press, 1976.

Martin, R.J. Dealing with criticism, *Learning*, March 1979, 92-93.

Martin, R.J. Focus on self: An approach to using Dreikursian principles to cope with power struggles in the classroom. *The individual psychologist*, 1979, *16* (2), 25-30.

Martin, R.J. Guilt feelings and guilt-evoking behavior. *The individual psychologist.* 1979, No. 4, 17-22.

Martin, R.J. *Teaching through encouragement.* Englewood Cliffs, New Jersey: Prentice-Hall, Inc., 1980.

Perls, F.S. *Gestalt therapy verbatim.* New York: Bantam Books, Inc., 1969.

Rogers, C.R. *Counseling and psychotherapy.* Boston: Houghton-Mifflin, 1942.

Rogers, C.R. *Client-centered therapy.* Boston: Houghton-Mifflin, 1951.

Rogers, C.R. *Freedom to learn.* Columbus, Ohio: Chas. E. Merrill, 1969.

Rowe, M.B. *Wait-time and reward as instructional variables, their influence on language, logic, and fate control:* Part one—Wait-time. Journal of Research in Science Teaching, 1974, 11, 81-94.

Smith, M.J. *When I say no, I feel guilty.* New York: Bantam Books, 1975.

Steiner, C.M. *Scripts people live.* New York: Bantam, 1974.

Von Foerster, H. On constructing a reality. *In Environmental design research*, Vol. 2. F.E. Preiser (Ed.). Stroudberg: Dowden, Hutchinson & Ross, 1973, 35-46.

Appendix: Synopsis of the skills and strategies

The following pages are a synopsis of all the skills and strategies and when to use them. You will find it a useful reference when you want to review any of the techniques discussed in this book.

SKILL ONE:
GIVING FEEDBACK BY REFLECTING

Basic Principle

> *Reflecting is an attempt to understand the total message—words, gestures, tone of voice, body language—and then to put that message into words.*

1. Paraphrasing: Restate the message using the speaker's language.

2. Summarizing: Summarize the message in a way which captures the essence of what the other person is saying.

3. Drawing implications: Put into words a message which is implied but not actually stated.

4. Literal repetition: Repeat key words and phrases when you want to let the other person know you are listening and to encourage the other person to continue.

SKILL TWO: RESPONDING NONVERBALLY

Basic Principle:

Responding nonverbally with attentive silence and listening cues encourages others to speak by letting them know you are listening.

1. Attentive silence: Wait (at least three seconds or longer) for others to continue at a pause in the conversation (increases quantity and quality of responses).

Sit or stand close enough to establish eye contact easily without invading the other person's personal space. (You will know if you have invaded others' personal space if they start edging away).

2. Listening cues: Break silences without commenting or asking questions by using words or sounds such as:

- Uh huh.
- Mm hmm.
- Yeah.
- Oh.
- I see.
- Go on.
- Continue.
- Tell me more.

(These words and noises have no substantive content, but they let the other person know you are listening, paying attention, and understanding.)

SKILL THREE: ASKING FOR SPECIFICS

Basic Principle:

Invite problem-centered responses by asking "What?" rather than "Why?"

The skill of *asking for specifics* allows you to get down to the specifics of what the problem is, what the alternatives are, and what people can do about the problem.

1. Questions which focus on specifics of the problem:

- What happened? [Focusing on the situation]
- What did you do? [Focusing on actions]
- How did (do) you feel about it? [Focusing on internal reaction]
- What is that . . . . (feedback vague phrases)? [Requesting others to be specific in their criticism]

2. Specifics of value judgments:

- Is what you are doing making things better or worse?
- Is what you are doing helping?

3. Specifics which focus on consequences:

- What will happen if . . . . (fill in alternative)?
- What is likely to happen?
- What is the worst possible thing that could happen?

4. Specifics which focus on what others want:

- What do you want?
- What do you want to happen?

5. Questions which focus on making plans and decisions:

- What can you do about it?
- What are you going to do about it?

6. Follow-up questions (use when answers to the above questions are not specific enough):

- Can you give an example? [Encouraging specifics]
- Can you be more specific? [Encouraging specifics]
- In what way? [Encouraging specifics]

SKILL FOUR:
I-STATEMENTS—GETTING ACROSS YOUR OWN CONCERNS, NEEDS, LIMITS, AND REACTIONS

Basic Principle

> When talking about your own problems, limits, reactions, and wants, use simple statements beginning with "I."

1. Expressing appreciation:

- I appreciate you for . . .
- I'm glad you . . .

2. Saying what you think without arguing:

- I think . . .

3. Setting limits by saying what you're willing to do:

- I am willing to . . .
- I'm not willing to . . .

4. Expressing anger and frustration:

- I feel frustrated by . . .
- I don't like it when . . .

5. Confronting others when you have a problem:

- When you do X, I feel Y because the effect on me is Z.

6. Accepting responsibility for mistakes:

- I am responsible for . . .
- That was my mistake . . .
- I made a mistake . . .

Appendix / 209

7. *Asking for what you want:*

- I want . . .
- I need . . .
- I would like . . .

8. *Expressing care, concern, and love:*

- I care.
- I'm concerned.
- I love you.
- I care what happens to you.

SKILL FIVE: FOCUSING ON AN AREA OF AGREEMENT

Basic Principle

If you refuse to fight, others cannot fight with you.

When others attempt to put you on the defensive, the skill of focusing on an area of agreement is useful in getting the other person to focus on the problem rather than on you.

1. Agreeing in part: Agree with that part of a statement which you can agree with, instead of disagreeing with an attack.

2. Giving information without contradicting: Answer an attack by stating what is true without contradicting the other person or making yourself a target.

3. Admitting mistakes: Meet an attack which is substantially true by admitting your mistakes without acting defensive.

STRATEGY 1: LISTENING

When to Use

1. The other person has the problem.
2. The other person wants you to listen or you are not sure what the other person wants.
3. You are willing to listen.

Goals

1. Establishing rapport.
2. Getting the other person involved (motivation).
3. Get information you need to proceed.
4. Give yourself time to make a decision.

The Strategy

Use Skills 1 (reflecting) and 2 (responding non-verbally) to:

1. Reflect the other person's main message.
2. Respond non-verbally with attentive silence and listening cues.

STRATEGY 2: HELPING OTHERS THINK THROUGH PROBLEMS

When to Use

1. The other person has the problem.
2. The other person wants someone to act as a sounding board in thinking through the problem.
3. You are willing to help the other person think through the problem.

Goal

Help the other person think through a problem where you want to supply a minimum of direction.

Use Skill 1 (Reflecting) To:

1. Reflect the specifics of the problem.
2. Reflect value judgments.
3. Reflect alternatives.
4. Reflect decisions.

STRATEGY 3: GETTING OTHERS TO ACCEPT RESPONSIBILITY

When To Use

1. The other person has the problem.
2. The other person wants help or at least agrees to interact with you.
3. You have a responsibility to confront the other person in regard to the problem.

Goal

Encourage others to accept responsibility and make decisions.

The Strategy

Use skill 2 (Asking for Specifics) to:

1. Identify specifics of the problem.
2. Get a value judgment.
3. Generate alternatives.
4. Ask for a decision.

STRATEGY 4: NEGOTIATING WHEN YOU HAVE A PROBLEM

When to Use

1. You have a problem. Even if the other person is the cause of the problem, if you are the one affected, you have the problem.

2. You want the other person to make a change which will help solve the problem.
3. You are willing to ask for what you want and/or are prepared to set limits.

Goals

1. Solve your own problems.
2. Maintain co-operative relationship with the other person.

The Strategy

Use Skill 1 (Reflecting) and Skill 4 (Making I-statements) to:

1. State the problem and/or ask for what you want using I-statements.
2. Listen and clarify the other person's position using reflection (as many times as necessary).
3. Restate and/or modify your own position using I-statements (as many times as necessary).
4. Agree on a solution.

STRATEGY 5: STAYING PROBLEM-CENTERED WHEN ATTACKED

When to Use

1. You have the problem of someone attacking you or attempting to engage you in a power struggle. You don't have to like or agree with the attack; you do need to cope with it.
2. You want to turn the attack into a problem-centered discussion.
3. You are willing to discuss the problem but not to engage in a fight or give in.

Goals

1. Stay problem-centered when under attack.
2. Avoid acting defensive under attack.
3. Get discussion onto the problem instead of the person.

The Strategy

Use the skills as necessary to:

1. Respond non-verbally until the other person finishes what he has to say.
2. Reflect the other person's concerns.
3. Focus on areas of agreement.
4. Ask for specifics of legitimate problems or criticisms.
5. Use I-statements to set limits without fighting or giving in.

Index

Actions, responsibility for, 176-77
Adjustment, 171
Advice, ineffective, 25
Agreeing in part, 87-89
Agreement, skill of focusing on, 86-92
  (see also Focusing on agreement)
Alberti, R.E., 74, 84
Alternatives:
  generating, 6, 133
  limited, 133-34
  in reflecting, 111, 116, 117
  skills as, 35
  to talking, 53
Anger, expressing, 78-79
Anthony, W.A., 41
Anxiety, 165 (see also Feelings)
Apologizing, 161
Appreciation, expressing, 74-76
Argument:
  avoiding, 87
  logical, 29
Asking for specifics, skill of, 58-72, 206-207
  in strategies, 123-133, 142, 144-45, 153-54, 157-58, 160
Asking for wants, 82-84 (see also I-statements)
Authier, J., 38, 39, 41, 52
Awareness:
  in choosing techniques, 199
  of preconceptions, 200

Bandler, R., 70, 197
Bassin, A., 120
Behavior:
  evaluating, 199
  observing, 10
  responsibility for, 177-78
Beliefs, irrational, 54-55, 147-48, 161-62, 168-70
Berne, E., 32, 182
Blame, 19-20, 78, 88, 161, 176
Bolton, R., 9
Brammer, L.M., 38, 39
Brattler, T.E., 120

Caring:
  appeals to, 20
  as an excuse, 135
  expressing, 84
  false, 165, 169
  irrational, 193

Carkhuff, R.R., 41
Change:
  avoiding (see Beliefs, irrational)
  of behavior, 201
  long term, 199
  by others, 121, 175
Choosing:
  a course of action, 65-71
  for others, 135
  a response, 43-45, 201
  a strategy, 99-101
  what to respond to, 41-45
Clarifying (see also Listening; Reflecting)
  one's own thinking, 46
  other's thinking, 45, 139
Commitments, 191
Communication patterns, 2
Complaints, responding to, 151-53
Concern, 84, 135 (see also Caring)
Conformity, 172
Confrontation, coping with, 156-157 (see also Problem-centered, strategy of staying)
Confronting, 140-141
  reasons for avoiding, 147
  using I-statements, 79 (see also I-statements)
Congruent behavior, 195 (see also Nonverbal cues; Tone of voice)
Consequences, 135, 179
  unpleasant, 147
  worst possible, 68
Contradicting, how to avoid, 89-90
Control, encouraging, 177, 192
Cooperation:
  between equals, 186-87
  when giving help, 191
  in power struggles, 92
Cotler, S.B., 78
Criticism:
  in helping relationships, 158
  image-centered, 11-15
  questions in, 63-64
  responding to, 157-160
Cues, listening (see Listening cues)

Decisions (see also Alternatives; Value judgments)
  asking for, 6, 123-24, 128, 131
  gaining time for, 95
  reflecting, 112
  responsibility for, 177

Defensiveness, 151, 160, 162
Demonstrating, 30–31
Dinkmeyer, D., 75
Discouragement, 166 (*see also* Image-centered criticism; Rescue game)
"Doing good," 173
Drawing implications, 40 (*see also* Reflecting)
  examples of, 105, 110, 111, 113–15, 117–18, 124–27
Dreikurs, R., 19, 75, 168, 176

Effectiveness:
  description, 2
  steps in learning, 2
  test of, 32
Egan, G., 41
Ellis, A., 12, 13, 19, 21, 68, 130, 132, 176
Emmons, M.L., 74, 85
Empathy, 28, 167 (*see also* Listening; Reflecting)
Encouragement (*see also* Praise)
  of control, 46
  of expression, 50
  of talk, 46, 95, 103
Equality, 192
Evaluation, positive, 15
Excuses, 161
Exercise for learning skills, 198
Expectations, 168, 172
Expertise:
  pretending to have, 192
  unwanted, 187–189
Eye contact, 50

Feedback, request for, 198 (*see also* Reflecting)
Feelings:
  of anxiety, 165
  of being victimized, 183–193
  reflecting, 41–42
  of responsibility, 180–81
  responsibility for, 176–79
  statement of, 81–82
Fisherman example, 186–187
Focusing on agreement, skill of, 86–92, 209
  in strategies, 122, 141–42, 144, 153, 155, 160
  techniques:
    admitting mistakes, 91
    agreeing in part, 87–89
    giving information, 89–91
Focusing on specifics (*see* Specifics)
Formulas in communicating, 198

Freire, P., 192
Frustration, 78 (*see also* Anger; Discouragement; Feelings)

Gazda, G.M., 120
Glasser, W., 120
Goals:
  of directive problem-solving, 120
  of listening, 95, 102
  of negotiating, 138
  of nondirective problem solving, 108
  of staying problem-centered, 150
Gordon, T., 52, 79–82, 97
Grinder, J., 70, 197
Grunwald, B., 168
Guerra, J.J., 78
Guidelines:
  for criticism, 12
  for getting other to accept responsibility, 135
  for learning skills and strategies, 194–201
  for listening, 107
  in negotiating, 148–49
  for praise, 19
  staying problem-centered, 160–61
Guilt, 11, 19–21, 165, 169

Hackney, H., 54, 58
Hall, E.T., 50
Harper, R.A., 13, 130
Helping:
  in behavior change, 121–123
  with criticism, 130–32
  with personal problems, 114
  with self-defeating attitudes, 128–29
  when unwilling, 191
Helping others think through problems, strategy of, 5, 108–119, 210–221
Hidden agendas, 42
Hints, dropping, 147
"Hired," getting, 123–24, 135, 140, 159

"I," when to avoid, 84–85 (*see also* I-statements)
Image-centered language, 8–32, 159 (*see also* Criticism; Praise)
  changing, 46
  defined, 8
  patterns, 9
I-message, Gordon's, 79–82
Impatience, communicating, 56
Implications, drawing, 40 (*see also* Reflecting)
Information:
  collecting, 95
  giving, 89–91